The Faithful Dove Flies Against The Wind

信鴿

迎風飛

The Faithful Dove
Flies Against The Wind

信鴿
迎風飛

Second Collection of Poems
詩詞第二集
1952-2012
A Chinese-English Bilingual Text
漢英對照

Br. Peter Zhou Bangjiu, O.S.B.
周 邦 舊 修 士

May 2013, First Edition
2013 年 5 月初版

January 2017, Second Edition
2017 年 1 月再版

St. Andrew's Abbey, USA
美國聖安德肋大修院

Printed in Taiwan
台灣印行

版　　　權：© 2013 和 2017 聖安德肋大修院。

審 訂 者：本院西滿・奧多尼爾神父（2007.12-2008.3），
　　　　　德肋撒・瑪利亞・莫洛女士（2008.12-2012.12）。

編　　　排：永望文化事業有限公司。

封 面 畫：尤金（辣法額爾）・薩蘭德拉 2008 年繪製。

封面裡照：艾琳・福爾斯 1993 年拍攝。

封底裡畫：尤金（辣法額爾）・薩蘭德拉 2008 年繪製。

封 底 照：1986 年 10 月 30 日，望完清晨彌撒後，在梵蒂岡
　　　　　宗座宮廷接見室，筆者向教宗若望保祿二世呈上
　　　　　了他的一冊《東方黎明在望》的英譯稿本，和他
　　　　　的關於聖父的四首賦於獄中的詩詞。

出 版 者：聖安德肋大修院，
　　　　　美國加利福尼亞州化野漠。

初　　　版：2013 年 5 月。

再　　　版：2017 年 1 月。

作　　　者：周邦舊。

書　　　名：信鴿迎風飛。

印　　　刷：台灣永望文化事業有限公司，
　　　　　台北市師大路 170 號 3 樓之 3，
　　　　　（02）23680350。

國際書號：978-986-5996-20-8（平裝本）。

Copyright: © 2013 and 2017 St. Andrew's Abbey.

Editors: Our Fr. Simon J. O'Donnell (12/2007-3/2008),
      Theresa Marie Moreau (12/2008-12/2012).

Layout: Yeong Wang Cultural Enterprise Company Ltd.

Cover Art: Eugene (Br. Raphael) Salandra in 2008.

Inside Front Cover Picture: Irene Foertsch in 1993.

Inside Back Cover Art: Eugene (Br. Raphael) Salandra in 2008.

Back Cover Picture: On October 30, 1986, after the morning Mass, in the audience room in the apostolic palace in the Vatican, Br. Peter presents Pope John Paul II with his English manuscript, *Dawn Breaks In The East*, and his four poems about the Holy Father composed in prison.

Publisher: St. Andrew's Abbey,
      P.O. Box 40, Valyermo, CA 93563, USA; 661-944-2178.

First Edition: In May 2013.

Second Edition: In January 2017.

Author: Br. Peter Zhou Bangjiu, O.S.B.

Title: The Faithful Dove Flies Against The Wind.

Printer: Yeong Wang Cultural Enterprise Company Ltd,
      3F-3, No 170 Shih Ta Road, Taipei, Taiwan, Republic Of China;
      (02) 23680350.

ISBN: 978-986-5996-20-8 (Softbound).

獻　詞

敬獻給基督之母聖瑪利亞

聖潔聰慧**瑪利亞**，
慈愛尊榮**基督母**。
訪晤表姊知奧秘，
高唱讚歌謝**上主**。

孺子衛教戰鬼怪，
終獲全勝賴祐助。
吟詩敘事抒胸臆，
勵己勵人頌**天父**。

敬獻詩詞近三百，
美化聖化祈賜予；
俾能頌**母**頌**主**愛，
滋潤肺腑益黎庶！

Dedication

To Saint Mary, Mother Of Christ

Mary,
Holy, pure and intelligent,
You are the loving-kind and honorable
Mother of Christ.
Visiting and seeing your cousin,
You knew the profound mystery
That you sang loudly a song of praise
To acknowledge your debt to the Lord.

I, your child,
Had ever fought the bogeys
In defense of the Church.
Depending on your help,
I ultimately had won an all-round victory.
I had even begun to compose poems,
To record events and to express my feelings,
On purpose
To encourage myself and others
And to laud our Heavenly Father.

I respectfully present to you nearly three hundred poems.
I plead for your beautifying and sanctifying,
So that they may be able to extol you, our Mother,
To praise the love of the Lord,
To soothe hearts,
And to benefit the people!

目　錄

Contents

前　言
戴米恩・托依洛洛大院長

聖安德肋大修院
2012 年 10 月 7 日
玫瑰聖母節

　　能為周修士的一本詩集書寫這篇前言，是我的榮幸。我開始認識周修士是在 1998 年，當我前來加入加利福尼亞州化野漠聖安德肋大修院這個修會團體時。那時，周修士是一個七十二歲的年輕人，十四年後的今天，他則是一個八十六歲的青年。他現在仍像我初次見到的一樣，精力充沛、行動敏捷、意志堅定。

　　見到周修士每晚飯後出外散步，誦念玫瑰經，這並非是罕見的事，這是他對榮福聖母的敬禮。另一件少見的事，是看到周修士用餐時，扮演的是修院服務員，而不是他本來的修院年長者的角色。他在自己實際上坐下進食前，總是在飯廳巡視，要對客人和修士桌上都有足夠的飲用水確信無疑。這使我想起了聖經中的一節：

> 「（耶穌問）是誰大呢？是坐席的，還是服事人的？
> 不是坐席的嗎？可是我在你們中間卻像是服事人
> 的。」
> （路 22：27）

　　儘管周修士有些靦腆，有些拘謹，但還是易於和他交談，也不會對他所擁有的精神力量和滿懷信心產生誤解。這無庸置疑，既是源於他在共產黨監獄二十六年的倖存的親身經歷，就

Foreword

Father Abbot Damien Toilolo, O.S.B.

St. Andrew's Abbey
October 7, 2012
Our Lady of the Rosary

It is an honor and privilege for me to write this foreword for Brother Peter's book of a collection of poems. I came to know Brother Peter when I joined the monastic community of St. Andrew's Abbey, Valyermo, California in 1998. At that time, Brother Peter was a young man of seventy-two years. Now, fourteen years later, he is a young man of eighty-six. He is as energetic, active and unwavering as he was when I first met him.

It is not unusual to see Brother Peter go out each night for his evening walk after dinner to pray his rosary; such is his devotion to our Blessed Mother. It is also not unusual to see Brother Peter during meals take on the role of a servant of the community, rather than an elder in the community, which he is. Before he himself actually sits down to eat, he makes his rounds in the refectory (dining room), making sure that both the guests and the monks have enough water at their tables. It reminds me of a passage in Scripture:

> "[Jesus asked] For which is the greater, one who sits at table, or the one who serves? Is it not the one who sits at table? But I am among you as one who serves." (Luke 22:27)

Despite his tendency to be shy and reserved, when one engages Brother Peter in conversation which is easy to do, there is no mistake of the interior strength and confidence he possesses. It undoubtedly comes from a life of deep prayer and solitude, as well as his personal experience of surviving twenty-six yeas in the Communist prisons as recounted in his book, *Dawn Breaks in the East*.

如他在自己的《東方黎明在望》的書中所敘述的那樣，也是源於一種深沉祈禱和寂然獨居的生活。

在這冊詩詞中，讀者要見到那些周修士賦於獄中，但實際上卻是並未用紙和筆寫下的詩詞，他牢牢地記住了成千首詩詞，而這些詩詞就有助於他心思的專注和集中。在那首談到他已記住兩千首詩詞的《小監三月》的詩中，他寫道：

「冀望記憶猶強勁，

保舊吟新增主光！」

本書證實了他恰好是那樣作的。而且，本書還以強大有力和深具影響的方式，在周修士傳佈福音訊息的同時，也一併讓世人知道他的不幸的但卻是英雄般的故事。正如天主利用耶穌在十字架上的醜惡、兇暴和殘酷的死亡，給了無生機的世界帶來了生命一樣。祂也利用周修士的事蹟和著作，來激勵和啓發世界人民。他的那些賦於鐵窗的黑暗中的詩詞，現已脫穎而出，顯露於光明和生活的自由中。

透過這些寫得很美麗的詩詞，讀者將會瞥見這位恬靜安詳的準殉道者的心靈深處，並且分享他的信德、虔敬和靈感。這些以樸實無華、清晰開朗的文筆寫出的詩詞，涵蓋了人類的感情從讚頌和歡樂到憂傷和悲痛的波動的幅度。而這正好有助於，使之容易接近讀者，由是邀請和鼓勵他或她，檢查、沉思與反省自身的信仰旅程和對天主的忠誠老實。

對周修士信德的服膺和仰賴，這冊詩詞和《東方黎明在望》，就是一個深刻的見證。他生命中的英勇事件，是教會初期的聖人和殉道者的生活和死亡事蹟的迴響。關於這些課題，對普通基督徒來說，都只能像白日做夢一樣地予以幻想罷了！

In this book of poems, the reader will encounter the actual poems Brother Peter 'wrote' in prison without the use of a pen or paper. He committed to memory thousands of poems, which helped to keep his mind occupied and focused. In his poem, *Three Months in a Solitary Cell,* in which he refers to having memorized two thousand poems, he writes:
"I Wish my memory to remain strong to keep the old poems
and compose new ones for the greater glory of God."

This book is evident that he did just that. It is another powerful and influential way in which Brother Peter simultaneously shares his unfortunate yet heroic story with the world while spreading the Gospel message. Just as God used the ugly, violent and cruel death of Jesus on the cross to bring life to a dead world, so He is using Brother Peter's story and writings to give encouragement and inspiration to people around the world. His poems which were composed in the darkness of prison, have now emerged into the freedom of light and life.

Through these beautifully written poems, the reader will be afforded a glimpse into the mind and heart of this quiet quasi-martyr. Brother Peter shares his faith, his devotions and inspirations in these poems. Written in an unpretentious and distinct style, these poems cover a range of human emotions: from praise and rejoicing to sorrow and lament. This is what helps to make these poems accessible to the reader and so invites and encourages him or her to examine, meditate and reflect upon their own journey of faith and their faithfulness to God.

This book of poems and *Dawn Breaks in the East* is a profound testimony to Brother Peter's conviction and confidence in the Faith. The heroic events of his life echo the stories of the lives and deaths of the early Church saints and martyrs; subjects about which the average Christian can only daydream about. Therefore, to have been given an opportunity to participate even in a small way in this book is both a humbling and privileged experience. I realize that few people in this world will ever have the opportunity and blessing that I have had to live, work and pray with Brother Peter on a daily basis, but the poems

因此，能有機會即使以微小的方式參與了本書，這既令我愧不
敢當，也令我覺得榮幸。我認爲在這個世界上少有人享有我所
享有的這種機緣和恩賜，天天與周修士一起生活、工作和祈禱；
不過，本書中的詩詞卻會對當今這位信仰鬥士的生活和靈修，
提供一些洞察和理解。

contained in this book, will provide some insight and understanding into the life and spirituality of this modern day champion of Faith.

序　文
周邦舊

聖安德肋大修院
2012 年 12 月 8 日
聖母無玷始胎節

　　1995 年 9 月詩詞初集出版後，第二集本來就應當發軔開
端；然而實際上，這項工作卻要推遲到 2007 年 8 月。在那段長
達 12 年的時期裡，我還得作出不懈的努力，來爲頭本書《**東方
黎明在望**》接踵而至的四次增訂本補充大批資料，並促使法文
譯本、中文原著甚至韓文譯本完成和出版。

　　這本集子蒐集了 275 首詩詞。頭 81 首詩詞是自 1978 年元
月初到 1981 年 7 月 22 日吟於獄中，記於心裡，後於 1985 年 1
月和 2 月在修院中寫於紙上。在這些 81 首詩詞中的最初 14 首，
是追憶一些發生在 1952 年 4 月 8 日到 1955 年 10 月 7 日之間的
事件，並以事件發生的日期作爲撰寫的日期。所有其他 194 首
詩詞，則是在 1981 年 7 月 25 日由鐵窗獲釋後，先吟於遂寧、
南充、成都和北京，後吟於東京和美國；而在我四次旅遊期間，
還吟於比利時、法國、義大利、梵蒂岡、中國大陸、台灣和香
港。

　　許多賦於獄中的詩詞需要改進，甚至需要重寫，以使其意
向和主旨清晰明確，節拍和音韻合乎格律。所有其餘的詩詞，
也需要更多的思考，更多的改善。每首詩詞的稿本一完成，英
譯文就得開始了。在翻譯的過程中，原稿有時需要改動，好使

Preface
Brother Peter Zhou Bangjiu, O.S.B.

St. Andrew's Abbey
December 8, 2012
Immaculate Conception of Mary

After the publication of the first collection of my poems in September 1995, the second collection should naturally have been started. Yet, in reality, the task had to be postponed to August 2007. During that 12-year period, I had to make unremitting efforts to supplement a great quantity of material to the following four revised editions of my first book, *Dawn Breaks In The East*, and to bring its French version, its Chinese original text and even its Korean version to completion and to be published.

The collection has gathered 275 poems. The first 81 poems had been composed in prison from early January 1978 to July 22 in 1981, kept in my mind, then written down on paper in the monastery in January and February 1985. The first 14 poems among the 81 poems recalled some events of the period from April 8, 1952 to October 7, 1955, and dated in accordance with the dates of the events. After my release from jail in July 25, 1981, all the other 194 poems were written in Suining, Nanchong, Chengdu, Beijing, then in Tokyo, and in the United States, and also, during my four travels to Belgium, France, Italy, the Vatican, Mainland China, Taiwan and Hong Kong.

A lot of the poems composed in prison needed to be improved, even to be recomposed so that their intentions and purposes might be clarified, and their meters and rhymes qualified. All the other poems also needed further consideration and more improvements. When the final draft of each poem was basically done, the English translation

其意蘊和思想更爲清澄。當譯稿積累到二十來篇時，我就得請人審改了。本院西滿・奧多尼爾神父，從 2007 年 12 月 3 日到 2008 年 3 月 2 日，共爲我審改了 64 首詩詞。自 1997 年 1 月到 2008 年 4 月離開修院，他一直就是我兩本書四次新版本的審訂者。德肋撒・瑪利亞・莫洛女士，從 2008 年 12 月直至現在，則爲我審改了所有其餘的 211 首詩詞。

2007 年 10 月，我有幸會見了，結識了德肋撒・瑪利亞・莫洛女士。2008 年 8 月，她開始志願地親切地審改了我那篇《歸國之行》的文章。自那時起，她就繼續修改了我的兩本書在兩次各自的增訂版中的所有補充資料和變動，而這還不包含審改詩詞。

德肋撒・瑪利亞・莫洛女士是一位有成就的記者和作家。近年來，她編輯和查考了一本書，書名叫《堅持信仰》，是關於中國聖母軍的創始人和推動者、愛爾蘭神父莫克勤，二十世紀五十年代初期在上海坐牢的事蹟。她還撰寫過其他多篇文章，就中有兩篇長文：一篇是涉及本院華倫士神父和我反抗中共宗教迫害的故事，另一篇是有關中國河北省懷來縣樊山鎮楊家坪熙篤會聖母神慰院的 33 位殉道者。這兩篇發表在《殘存者》上的文章，分別於 2010 年 6 月 27 日和 2011 年 6 月 26 日，自洛杉磯新聞俱樂部獲得了新聞頭等獎。

她對中國的歷史和文化曾有所研究，對之相當瞭解。她知道中國的現狀，她關懷受難的教會和遭到迫害的天主教徒。由於有著這些認識，興趣和情懷，她在閱讀我的文章和詩詞時，就能認清和洞悉我本來的意向、目的、思想、心境與情緒，就能容易地恰當地作出審訂。她修改我的稿件非常細心，她盡量

had to start. In the process of translating, the original text sometimes
had to be changed to make the meaning and the thought more clear.
When the translations of twenty or so poems were finished, I would
ask some one to help me with the editing. Our Fr. Simon J. O'Donnell
had edited 64 poems for me from December 3, 2007 to March 2, 2008.
He had been the editor of my two books in the four new editions since
January 1997, until his leaving the monastery in April 2008. Theresa
Marie Moreau did the editing for all the other remaining 211 poems
from December 2008 until the present.

I had the luck to meet Theresa Marie Moreau and make friends
with her in October 2007. In August 2008 she started to edit
voluntarily and graciously my article, *A Trip back to My Homeland*.
From then on, she continued revising all the supplementary materials
and changes of my two books in their two separate updated editions,
not including the poems.

Theresa Marie Moreau is a journalist and writer of achievements.
In the recent years, she edited and researched a book, *Perseverance
Through Faith* concerning the imprisonment in Shanghai in the early
1950s of the Rev. Fr. W. Aedan McGrath, an Irish priest and the
founder and promoter of the Legion of Mary in China. She has also
written many other pieces, including two long pieces: one regarding
the stories of our Fr. Eleutherius Winance and me resisting the
Chinese Communist religious persecution, and the other one regarding
the 33 Martyrs of the Cistercian Abbey of Our Lady of Consolation at
Yangjiaping in Fanshan Township in Huailai County in Hebei
Province, China. These two pieces were published in *The Remnant*
and both received first place journalism awards from the Los Angeles
Press Club on June 27, 2010 and on June 26, 2011.

She has researched and known quite well the Chinese history and
culture. She has been aware of the current situation in China and

使每字、每句、每個成語和每個格言都完全正確，易讀易懂，十分清楚，甚至相當優雅。一般說來，每首詩詞都需要審查兩三次，間或甚且四五次。有些時候我還應當接受她的建議，變更某些原來的字眼、措詞和表達方式，以使詩詞更加優美、更加生動、更加有力、更加強勁。在審改中，她顯示了自己的智慧、洞察力、耐心和熱忱。這本集子或可稱爲我們兩人四年來艱苦努力的共同創作。現在，我希望讀者細細賞閱，徐徐玩味。當然，我也應該期望讀者不吝指正，惠賜教言，因爲就如一首格言所說的那樣：金無足赤，人無完人。

　　本書還插入了 93 張本人和親友的照片。照片排列的順序，是按其拍攝日期的先後。頭 48 張置於 102 首詩詞之後，其餘的則尾隨 195 首詩詞。

　　本書裡所有的中國人名和地名的音譯詞，是按照《漢語拼音》拼寫的，但也有兩個例外：香港和台北。

　　賦於獄中並已於 1985 年初抄錄於紙的詩詞，尙有 600 來首還在小筆記本裡酣睡著。我想在自己寥寥無幾、屈指可數的殘餘歲月裡，我應當設法將它們喚醒。由於我今天的生命，既像風中之燭，也像西下夕陽，我不知道酣睡中的詩詞，究竟有多少可以被喚醒而得見天日。只有天主才曉得！對我來說，只要自己陷於困境中的視力容許，只要其他一切主觀方面的可能性仍然存在，我就要把這項工作向前推進。

　　這冊詩詞第二集現在終於面世了，但其面世絕不是靠我自己的能力，而是靠上主的慈愛和恩寵，靠祂鼓動了許多人向我伸出了援手，靠這些向我伸出過援手者，同時也靠聖母的幫助。爲此，我應當向慈主感恩，向聖母感恩，向長達四年耐心審稿

concerned about the suffering Church and the persecuted Catholics. Owing to her knowledge, interest and feelings, wheen reading my articles and poems, she could realize and understand well my original intentions, purposes, thoughts, moods and emotions, and do the edits easily and appropriately. She revised my pages very attentively and tried her best to make every word, sentence, idiom and maxim fully correct, understandable and clear, even elegant. Generally speaking, every poem needed to be examined twice or thrice, yet sometimes even four or five times. At times, I should accept her suggestions to change certain original words, wordings and the ways of expressing to make the poems more graceful, more vivid, more vigorous and more powerful. In the editing she has shown her wisdom, insight, patience and zeal. This collection might be called a creation of our joint arduous efforts for four years! Now, I would hope the reader will read appreciatively and ponder slowly. But, of course, I should also hope that you, my reader, will feel free to give your comments and to be so kind as to grant your advice; for like a maxim says: There is no pure gold in the world, nor is there a perfect man.

In this book there are also inserted 93 photos of myself, my relatives and friends. They are arranged according to the order of the times when they were taken. The first 48 placed after the 102nd poem, and the rest, after the 195th poem.

The Hanyu Pinyin is used for the transliterations of all Chinese personal names and place names in the book, but with two exceptions, Hong Kong (Xianggang) and Taipei (Taibei).

There are still over 600 poems, composed in prison and copied down on paper in early 1985. They are still sleeping soundly in my little notebooks. I thought I should try to wake them up during my remaining so few years to be counted on my fingers. Since my life of today is like a candle fluttering in the wind or like the setting sun in

的德肋撒・瑪利亞・莫洛女士感恩，向本院爲審稿半年的西滿・奧多尼爾神父感恩，向爲本書撰寫《前言》的本院戴米恩・托伊洛洛大院長感恩，向爲繪兩幅美術畫的尤金・薩蘭德拉先生（前本院辣法額爾修士）感恩，向所有爲本書提供了照片的親友感恩。最後，我還應向爲本書打字、編排和印刷的台灣永望文化事業有限公司感恩致謝。

2016 年 8 月 15 日

聖母蒙召升天

　　在這次的第二版中，只有些微更動，而這點更動也曾由德肋撒・瑪利亞・莫洛女士惠爲審訂。

the west, I do not know how many of the sleeping poems will be awakened and see the light of day. Only God knows! For my part, I will forge ahead to work on them as long as my eyesight, which is in trouble, permits and all the other subjective possibilities still exist.

This second collection of my poems now finally appears. Its appearance, however, has never depended on my own capacity, but on the love and favor of the Lord, on His moving many people to lend me their helping hands; and on the assistance of Our Lady. On account of this, I must acknowledge my debt to the loving Lord, to Our Holy Mother, to Theresa Marie Moreau for her editing so patient and so long as for four years, to our Fr. Simon J. O'Donnell for his editing for half a year, to our Fr. Abbot Damien Toilolo for his Foreword to the book, to Mr. Eugene (Br. Raphael) Salandra for his two pieces of art, to my relatives and friends for their providing the photos, and ultimately, to the Yeong Wang Cultural Enterprise Company, Ltd. in Taiwan for the typing, layout and printing of the book.

August 15, 2016

Assumption of the Blessed Virgin Mary

Only little changes were made in this second edition; and the changes were kindly edited by Theresa Marie Moreau.

1. 徐樂君神父於當眾宣讀　　教宗庇護十二世通諭前　　在聖堂被拘捕

憶秦娥
成都
1952 年 4 月 13 日
復活節

頌書簡，
教宗衛**教紅魔**譴。
紅魔譴，
陰謀戳破，
信徒嘉勉。

徐乘彌撒堂中獻，
即將宣讀傳書簡。
傳書簡，
知情警到，
捕忠招叛！

1.   Fr. Thomas Xu Lejun Is Arrested In The Church Just Before His Reading Out In Public The Encyclical Letter *Cupimus Imprimis* By Pope Pius XII

To the Tune of Yi Qin E
(Remembering the Beauty of Qin)
Chengdu
April 13, 1952
Easter Sunday

The Pope issued an encyclical letter
To defend the Church
And to condemn the Red devils.
IN condemning the Red devils,
He laid bare their conspiracy
And also praised and encourged the faithful.

Seizing the opportunity
Of offering the Mass in his church,
Fr. Thomas Xu was about
To read out and spread the letter.
Having alrady received information
About his forthcoming spreadng the letter,
The policemen entered
To arrest the loyal
And to call the traitors!

2. 喜獲廣州
福壽康神父回信

浣溪沙
遂寧
1952 年 7 月

兩度修書非枉然，
回音今獲喜心間，
未提所望有何干？

字跡表明為外籍，
法文擬用復書翰，
要求願望再明言。

2.   Receiving Joyously A Reply From Fr. Pierre Narbais-Jaureguy Of Guangzhou

To the Tune of Huan Xi Sha
(Yarn Washed in the Stream)
Suining
July 1952

It is not useless
That I wrote to him twice.
Now,
Getting his reply,
There is rejoicing in my heart.
What does it matter
That my wishes have not been mentioned?

The Handwriting indicates his foreign nationality.
I intend to write back to him in French,
And I will say openly once more
My requests and my wishes.

3. 《告全國神職人員和教友書》
文稿
遙寄廣州和上海

浪淘沙
遂寧
1952 年 9 月 21 日

文稿訂重新，
抄寫勞神，
隨函今寄穗和申。
祝願一帆風順到，
求主施恩。

赤縣湧風雲，
教會蒙塵，
眾多兄妹困心身。
真相認清齊衛**教**，
期望殷殷！

3.   Mailing To The Very Remote Cities, Guangzhou and Shanghai, My Manuscript
Letter To The Clergy And Laity Of The Church In China

To the Tune of Lang Tao Sha
(Wave-Washed Sands)
Suining
September 21, 1952

The manuscript has been revised once more;
I exerted my strength in transcribing.
Today, I mailed it along with
A letter separately to Guangzhou and Shanghai.
I wish it reaches there in plain sailing,
Praying the Lord for granting this favor.

A storm has been surging in China,
Leading the Church covered with dust,
And embarrassing many brothers and sisters
In mind and body.
Seeing clearly the facts
And defending together the Church:
This is my earnest expectations for them!

4. 謝懷鈞老闆問道

四言詩
遂寧
1952 年 11 月 21 日

中年謝君，髮店主人；
技藝精湛，顧客盈門。

與父交往，已逾十春；
父攤賣鏡，緊靠店門。

我坐攤邊，默念經文；
他來閒聊，面佈愁雲。

店內事務，問題紛紜；
與僱工處，令之傷神。

人生正道，他欲探詢；
簡言以對，知其難遵。

天變**教**危，狼嚎民呻；
真善縱知，有誰敢跟？

4. Mr. Xie Huaijun, A Boss, Seeks The Right Way

In the Poetic Style of Siyan Shi
Suining
November 21, 1952

Mr. Xie, a middle-aged man,
Is the owner of a barbershop.
His superb skill
Attracts customers to crowd his shop.

He has associeted with my father
For over ten springs.
My father's stall for selling eyeglasses
Is very close to the shop's doors.

When I sit by the side of the stall,
Reciting my prayers in silence,
He came to me for a chat,
With a melancholy look.

In the affairs of the shop
The problems are diverse and confused;
To get along with the hired workers,
He feels distressed and sad.

Concerning the right way of life
He wants also to inquire of me.
I gave him only a very simple answer,
Thinking and knowing
That it is not easy for him to observe.

The sky has changed,
The Church has been in danger,
The wolves howl,
And the people groan.
Is there someone,
Though knowing well the truth and the goodness,
Who has the courage to follow?

5. 福壽康神父
和瑪利亞·加辣修女
收到公函的通知

如夢令
遂寧
1952 年 11 月 27 日

穗滬回函終到，
欣悉均收文稿。
法譯本將成，
福且佳音傳報。
聞耗，
聞耗，
續戰虎狼獅豹！

5. The Acknowledgments Of My Open Letter From Fr. Pierre Narbais-Jaureguy And Sr. Marie-Claire

To the Tune of Ru Meng Ling
(Like a Dream)
Suining
November 27, 1952

The replies from Guangzhou and Shanghai
Have arrived at last.
I rejoice over learning
That both of them had received the manuscripts.
About the French translation
Already on the point of completion,
Fr. Pierre,
Moreover,
Comunicates to me the welcome news.
Hearing the news,
Hearing the news,
I must continue fighting
Tigers, wolves, lions and leopards!

6. 寫作到深夜

浣溪沙
遂寧
1953 年 1 月 25 日

慈父醒來燈見燃，
兩回勸我上床眠。
我仍寫到夜闌珊。

儘以脣舌**公教**衛，
猶須撰稿斥讕言。
崇高志趣欲沖天！

6. Writing Late Into The Night

To the Tune of Huan Xi Sha
(Yarn Washed in the Stream)
Suining
January 25, 1953

Waking up from sleep,
My loving father
Sees my oil lamp still burning;
He urges me
To go to bed, to sleep.
Yet,
I remain writing to the depths of night.

Having defended
The Catholic Church with words,
I should still write
To denounce calumnies.
My noble interests
Soar into the skies!

7. 獲瑪利亞-加辣修女回信

減字木蘭花
遂寧
1953 年 2 月 10 日

難於去國，
家裡蝸居腸百結。
就讀申城，
加辣致函請說情。

回音今獲，
無證院方難允諾。
何必憂愁？
福鐸證明能為求。

7.   Receiving A reply From Sr. Marie-Claire

To the Tune of Jian Zi Mulan Hua
(The Magnolia)
Snining
February 10, 1953

It is difficult for me
To leave the country;
Living in a small home,
I am weighed down with anxiety.
To go to the city of Shanghai to study,
I have sent to Sr. Marie-Claire a letter,
Asking her to intercede for me.

Today,
I received her reply
Informing me
That the seminary authorities will
Rarely give permission without certification.
What is there to be depressed?
Fr. Pierre Narbais-Jaureguy
Can help get the certification for me.

8. 會晤遠親外姪女陳趄

浪淘沙
遂寧
1953 年 4 月 4 日

兩載住同房，
記憶猶香。
念年暌別換容裝。
紅面柳腰嬌體態，
隨逝時光！

事母又經商，
久已居孀。
購齊貨物即還鄉。
祈把經文黃鐸獻，
祐爾穹蒼！

8.   A Meeting With Chen Chao, My Distant Niece

To the Tune of Lang Tao Sha
(Wave-Washed Sands)
Suining
April 4, 1953

We lived together in the same house
For Two years.
This remains sweet in my memory.
After a separation of twenty years,
Your face and clothing have changed.
Your rosy cheeks, pretty face,
Slender waist and graceful posture,
All these have passed away
Along with years!

You have taken care of your mother
And engaged in business;
You have been long since widowed.
Having purchased all your goods,
You are on the point of
Returning to your native place.
Please present to Fr. Huang
The prayer by Pope Pius XII.
Heaven bless you!

9. 劉修女勸我參加
宗教學習會

浪淘沙
遂寧
1953 年 4 月 11 日

黃鐸進監門，
轉瞬三春，
群羊無牧歧途奔，
目擊災殃堂口受，
五內如焚。

修女訪紆尊，
兜售「革新」，
參加學習勸諄諄。
辯解託詞當面駁，
正氣凌雲。

9.   Sr. Liu Persuades Me To Join The Religious Study Meetings

To the Tune of Lang Tao Sha
(Wave-Washed Sands)
Suining
April 11, 1953

Fr. Huang Hairuo has been put behind bars
For three springs, in a flash.
The flock without a shepherd
Takes a wrong path.
Witnessing the disaster-stricken parish,
I am torn by deep anxiety!

Condescending to pay me a visit,
The nun peddles to me the "reformation"
And persuades me tirelessly
To join the study meetings.
I reject her explanations and excuses
To her face,
With my spirit soaring to the heavens!

10. 文嘉禮院長的證明

清平樂
遂寧
1953 年 6 月 15 日

回函收暢，
福鐸佳音饗：
已給證明文院長，
且已申城寄往。

讀書赴滬艱難，
剛剛跨過頭關。
願望縈迴腦際，
猶求慈主成全！

10.   The Certification
From Fr. Prior Raphael Vinciarelli

To the Tune of Qing Ping Yue
(The Qing Ping Song)
Suining
June 15, 1953

I am happy to receive a reply
From Fr. Pierre Narbais-Jaureguy.
I enjoy with the good news:
The certificate has been already
Given by Fr. Prior Raphael Vinciarelli
And mailed to the city of Shanghai.

It is difficult for me
To go to Shanghai to study;
I have just crossed the first checkpoint.
My wishes still linger in my mind;
I have to implore the merciful Lord
To help accomplish them!

11. 城關派出所
拒發遷移證

四言詩
遂寧
1953 年 8 月 28 日

上海修女，為我面懇，
赴滬讀書，主教終允。

近獲匯款，證件回信；
大致寫好，「天堂」稿本。

派出所門，兩度走進，
遷滬申請，竟拒批准。

謀劃一年，心思費盡；
福鐸修女，齊來指引。

事敗何嘆？精神重振；
繼續為主，衝鋒陷陣！

11.   The Chengguan Police Station Refuses To Issue A Certification For Moving

In the Poetic Style of Siyan Shi
Suining
August 28, 1953

The nun in Shanghai
Implores the Bishop to his face
For my going to study in Shanghai;
The Bishop finally granted the permission.

Recently,
I received a remit, the certification and a reply.
My manuscript *From Paradise To Purgatory*
Has been written approximately well.

Entering twice the gates of the police station,
I applied for moving to Shanghai,
But I was unexpectedly denied the ratification.

I have contrived this matter for one year,
And racked my brains;
Fr. Pierre Narbais-Jaureguy and Sr. Marie-Claire,
Each came to give me their guidance.

For this failure
Why should I sigh?
Instead,
I must rebrace up
And continue fighting bravely for the Lord!

12. 江懋剛先生被捕

七律

成都

1954 年 10 月 7 日

半年相識憶猶歡，
尊府初登七日前。
國破民惶愁臆滿，
魔高道降憤膺填。
代還聖籍夫人至，
聞進黑牢戰友酸。
迫害今遭茹苦楚，
豪情鬥志冀望堅！

12.   The Arrest of Mr. Jiang Maogang

In the Poetic Style of Qilu
Chengdu
October 7, 1954

I remain glad in my memory
Of being acquainted with you for half a year.
Seven days before,
I called at your house the first time.
About the country defeated and subjugated,
And about the people alarmed and scared,
You have anxiety in your heart.
Against the rising of the evil and the false,
And against the falling of the good and the right,
You have resentment in your breast.
From Mrs. Jiang, your beloved wife,
Who comes here to give back the holy books for you,
Learning your entering into the black dungeon,
I, as a battle companion of yours,
Feel very, very sorrowful!
Now,
You suffer persecution and eat bitterness;
I wish you keeping firmly
Your lofty spirit and fighting will!

13. 惠立民醫生
探問共諜事件

減字木蘭花
成都
1955 年 9 月 9 日

近方知悉，
共諜五年忠裡匿。
君亦風聞，
害教詳情來探詢。

莫驚莫憤，
麥稗同田慈主訓，
警惕提高，
續衛漁船戰怒濤！

13.   Dr. Hui Limin Inquires About The Case Of The Communist Spies

To the Tune of Jian Zi Mulan Hua
(The Magnolia)
Chengdu
September 9, 1955

Just recently
We have learned
That the Communist spies have hidden themselves
Among us, the loyal ones, for five years.
Learning this also through hearsay,
You come to find out
The details of their harming the Church.

We must not be astonished
Or be angry;
About the wheat and weeds
In the same field.
There has been an instruction
From the merciful Lord.
Heightening our vigilance,
We should continue
Defending the Fishing Boat
And fighting against the raging billows!

14. 與劉懷琦小姐晤談

菩薩蠻
成都
1955 年 10 月 7 日

家人離境隻身處，
政權紅色難趨附。
工作實無緣，
境艱志氣狷。

晤談來下午，
共謀君憎惡。
嚮往主耶穌，
來朝領洗舒！

14.   A Talk With Miss Liu Huaiqi

To the Tune of Pusa Man
(Strange Goddess)
Chengdu
October 7, 1955

Since your family left the country,
You have lived all alone.
It was hard for you
To curry favor with the Red regime.
You have no chance
To get a job.
Your circumstances are arduous,
But your ambitions are upright.

This afternoon
You came here to talk with me.
You detest the Communist spies.
You yearn for Jesus, Our Lord;
One day in the future,
When you are baptized,
You will be happy!

15. 聽關於
《中美建交聯合公報》的廣播

水調歌頭
蓬安勞改營
1978 年 12 月 20 日

棄友交仇敵，
羞郝白宮顏。
孤台且獲益友，
雀躍海中南。
「開放」聲音響遍，
經濟興隆在望，
貿易好機緣。
失誤念餘夏，
易轍乃當然。

箝言論，
控媒體，
限人權，
卅年已逝，
大陸行事一如前。
眼見友邦背棄，
耳聽敵人歡唱，
台北茹辛酸。
望續行仁政，
鎮靜渡難關！

15. Listening To The Broadcast Regarding
The Joint Communique On The Establishment Of The Diplomatic Relations Between China And The USA

To the Tune of Shui Diao Ge Tou
(The Song of the Water Music)
Peng'an Labor-Reform Camp
December 20, 1978

Abandoning its friend to associate with the enemy,
The White House must blush with shame.
Isolating Taipei and winning a helpful friend,
The Zhongnanhai must jump for joy.
The sound of "Opening-up" is ringing there all over,
The prosperity of the economy is coming in view,
And the good chance for trade is arriving.
The error has lasted for more than twenty summers;
It is only natural
That the White House gets out of the old ruts.

Pinning down the speech.
Gagging the media,
And limiting human rights,
After a lapse of thirty years,
The Mainland conducts itself as usual.
Seeing the friendly nation deserting,
Hearing the enemy singing merrily,
Taipei eats bitterness.
We wish it will
Continue carrying out the policies of benevolence
And keep calm to tide over the difficulty!

16. 聽關於
《中共十一屆三中全會公報》
的廣播

采桑子
蓬安勞改營
1978 年 12 月 22 日

十年「文革」災深重，
無數冤魂。
禍首誰人？
毛躺晶棺猶似神！

「鬥爭綱領」今停用，
除舊更新。
「建設」重申，
強國之林欲廁身！

16.   Listening To The Broadcast Regarding *The Bulletin Of The Third Plenary Session Of The Chinese Communist Party*

To the Tune of Cai Sang Zi
(Picking Mulberries)
Peng'an Labor-Reform Camp
December 22, 1978

The catastrophe of the ten-year Cultural Revobution
Was extrenely serious,
Causing countless people wronged and becoming ghosts.
Who were the chief culprits?
Lying in a crystal sarcophagus,
Mao is still esteemed like a god!

The "guidelines of struggle"
Are no longer used;
Instead,
They should ring out the old
And ring in the new.
The "construction" is reaffirmed
To help the country
Take its place among the powerful nations!

17. 看電影《神秘旅客》

采桑子
蓬安勞改營
1978 年 12 月 23 日

北京美使基辛訪，
秘密神奇。
和解齊期，
共識達成彼此怡。

七年前事登螢幕，
欲世周知：
聯大身躋，
與美建交肇始茲。

17.   **Watching The Film**
The Mysterious Traveler

To the Tune of Cai Sang Zi
(Picking Mulberries)
Peng'an Labor-Reform Camp
December 23, 1978

The American envoy, Henry Kissinger
Paid a visit to Beijing
In a secret and mysterious way.
Expecting the reconciliation,
The two sides took delight
In reaching an agreement.

The matter seven years before was
To appear on the screen
And to be acknowledged publicly:
Ranking the United Nations General Assembly
And establishing the diplomatic relations wth the USA,
Both started on this matter.

18. 向主辭歲

臨江仙
蓬安勞改營
1978 年 12 月 31 日

新老**教宗**同月逝，
接班主教波蘭。
北京詛咒有何干？
暗**中俄共**助，
數國變紅天。

僅僅一回評審受，
年終安渡難關。
賦詩亦樂亦辛酸。
蒙恩深謝**主**，
辭歲滿心歡！

18. Seeing Off The Old Year Before The Lord

To the Tune of Lin Jiang Xian
(Immortal by the River)
Peng'an Labor-Reform Camp
December 31, 1978

The old and the new Popes
Died in the same month,
And the bishop from Poland succeeded.
What business of the Church
Is the curse from Beijing?
Because with the secret assistance
Of the Russian Communist Party,
The skies of several countries have become Red!

Appraised only once,
I got through unscathed
The year-end barrier.
In composing poems,
I have felt both joyous and painful.
Deeply grateful to the Lord for His favors,
I am filled wih joy
In bidding farewell to the old year!

19. 元旦祝願

西江月
蓬安勞改營
1979 年 1 月 1 日

寒氣**燕山**下降，
春風仍沐**玉山**。
福音雨露灑塵寰，
萬國萬民親善！

英語重溫順利，
詩詞續賦餘閒。
昂揚鬥志悉如前，
向**主**恭呈良願！

19.   Wishes On New Year's Day

To the Tune of Xi Jiang Yue
(Moon over the West River)
Peng'an Labor-Reform Camp
January 1, 1979

The cold air in Yanshan may diminish;
Yushan will still bathe in the spring breeze.
The Gospel will spray its rain and dew
All over the world.
So all the nations and people
May live friendly with each other!

It may be smooth for me
To review my English.
I will continue
Composing my new poems at my leisure.
My militant fervor
Will be high as usual.
I offer all these my good wishes
To the Lord reverently!

20. 看電影《天仙配》

浣溪沙
蓬安勞改營
1979 年 1 月 6 日

仙女配凡神話娟。
壓山子救慶團圓。
唱腔劍影扣心弦。

觸景生情慈主問：
娘親受壓為身翻，
何年何月倒華山？

20.   Watching The Movie
The Fairy Maiden's Marriage

To the Tune of Huan Xi Sha
(Yarn Washed in the Stream)
Peng'an Labor-Reform Camp
January 6, 1979

The fairy maiden married an earthly man;
This was a beautiful myth.
The maiden was punished
And compressed under a mountain, Huashan,
But rescued by her son
And had, finally, a happy reunion.
The melodies and the sword's glint and flash
Stir up the souls of watchers.

This scene aroused in me such a sense
As to ask the merciful Lord:
To help the oppressed Church, our Mother,
Being liberated,
In what year,
In what month,
Will the Huashan be overthrown?

21. 越共攻佔金邊

浪淘沙
蓬安勞改營
1979 年 1 月 11 日

越共佔金邊，
中共心酸，
徒孫暴政被推翻。
同樣害人三惡犬，
吵鬧喧天。

二百萬黎元，
僅僅三年，
或遭殺害或傷殘。
罪惡滔天嘗苦果，
柬共悽然！

21.   The Vietnamese Communists Striking and Capturing Phnom Penh

To the Tune of Lang Tao Sha
(Wave-Washed Sands)
Peng'an Labor-Reform Camp
January 11, 1979

Seeing Phnom Penh captured
By the Vietnamese Communists,
The Chinese Communists have felt sad,
For the tyranny of their spawns
Has been overthrown.
These three fierce dogs,
Equally harmful to the people,
Fill the air
With their mutual wrangles and quarrels.

Two million people,
Only during three years,
Were killed or injured.
Now,
From their own crimes reaching to the heavens
Tasting their own bitter fruit,
The Cambodian Communists are sorrowful!

22. 春節感懷

鷓鴣天
蓬安勞改營
1979 年 1 月 28 日

景象清新大治年，
監中鑼鼓亦喧闐。
神州天色仍陰暗，
「四化」籃圖枉絢爛。

松翠綠，
挺昂然，
頂天立地戰嚴寒，
隆冬縱使無窮盡，
屈膝迎春難上難。

22.   Some Thoughts On The Spring Festival

To the Tune of Zhegu Tian
(Partridges in the Sky)
Peng'an Labor-Reform Camp
January 28, 1979

The scene in this year of great order
Is refreshing;
The deafening sound of gongs and drums
Is also heard in the prison.
Yet the sky of China, the Divine Land,
Is still gloomy.
The blueprint of the Four Modernizations
May be georgeous in vain.

The emerald pine
Stands upright,
Fighting a battle against the icy cold,
With a dauntless spirit.
Even if the bitter winter is endless,
It will be extremely difficult for it
To go down on its knees,
To welcome the spring!

23. 致函香港李博嵐院長 請購英漢字典

菩薩蠻
蓬安勞改營
1979 年 3 月 12 日

蓉城兩月無回信，
存書果獄如灰爐。
鴻雁囑南飛，
寶書望帶歸。

多年忠照舊，
暗示諸良友。
他日盼重逢，
主恩求五中。

23.   A Letter To Fr. Prior Paulinus Li In Hong Kong, Asking For English-Chinese Dictionaries

To the Tune of Pusa Man
(Strange Goddess)
Peng'an Labor-Reform Camp
March 12, 1979

There is no answer for two months
From the city of Chengdu.
My books, kept in Nanchong Prison,
Vanished into ashes.
Now,
I urge the swan goose
To fly southward,
Expecting it to bring back to me precious books.

After many years,
My loyalty remains the same as before.
This is hinted to him, Fr. Prior,
And to all my other good friends.
I hope some day to meet them again.
For this favor
I appeal to the Lord from my heart!

24. 看戲曲片《尤三姐》

眼兒媚
蓬安勞改營
1979 年 3 月 17 日

隨風母姐任飄揚，
抗霸凱歌昂。
見疑於柳，
憤而自盡，
身死貞彰！

蓮花出自泥塘堰，
境窘豈頹唐？
持身純潔，
堅貞到底，
定綻花香！

24.   Watching A Documentory Film
You San Jie (Third Sister You)

To the Tune of Yan Er Mei
(The Eyes' Fascinaion)
Peng'an Labor-Reform Camp
March 17, 1979

Letting her mother and her elder sister
Fly with the wind,
Third Sister You determined
To fight against the evil power.
She sang finally a song of triumph
With a high spirit.
Because of being suspected
By Mr. Liu, her fiancé,
She was so angry as to kill herself.
She died,
But her virginity was made evident!

The lotus flower from bog
Has an awkward situation.
Could it be dejected?
When it is resolved
To behave purely and honestly,
And to remain faithful and staunch to the end,
It is sure to bloom
And give out fragrance of a flower!

25. 中共對越共
自衛還擊半月後
宣佈撤軍

醉花陰
蓬安勞改營
1979 年 3 月 20 日

略地攻城徒勇猛，
中共傷亡重。
柬共早奔逃；
仍佔金邊，
越共無惶恐。

寰球譴責如潮湧，
中共能無動？
「開放」不能停，
經濟當興，
撤退鑽心痛！

25.   After Half A Month Of Fighting Back Against The Vietnamese Communists In Self-Defence, The Chinese Communists declare The Withdrawal

To the Tune of Cui Hua Yin
(Tipsy in the Flowers' Shade)
Peng'an Labor-Reform Camp
March 20, 1979

In vain,
Taking cities and seizing territories
Courageously and powerfully,
The Chinese Communists have suffered heavy casualties.
The Cambodian Communists had run away long ago;
The Vietnamese Communists stll occupy Phnom Penh,
Not being terror-stricken.

Being have been lashed by the waves
Of condemnation from the whole world,
The Chinese Communists can be unmoved?
Moreover,
They should not stop their "open,"
And they should develop their economy.
Then,
Despite a feeling of acute sorrow,
They should withdraw their troops!

26. 獄友告以
我將被提名參與英語測驗

蝶戀花
蓬安勞改營
1979 年 3 月 31 日

科長週前嘗召問，
聲色俱溫英語詢詳盡。
案件加刑重審允，
定糾錯誤傳佳訊。

英語三囚教最近，
將與英文測驗聞音信。
垢辱長蒙無怨恨，
聲名鵲起何興奮！

26.   Fellow Prisoners Telling Me That I May Be Nominated To Join In Taking An English Test

To the Tune of Die Lian Hua
(Butterflies Courting Flowers)
Peng'an Labor-Reform Camp
March 31, 1979

One week ago,
The section chief called me in
For a talk.
Being mild in voice and countenance,
He inquired something
About my English in details.
He promised to help with getting a retrial
For the case of my last additional sentence.
He delivered to me a welcome message:
A wrong must be righted when found.

Recently,
I began to teach English
To three fellow prisoners.
I hear also some news:
I may participate in an English test.
Though having suffered shames and insults
For a long time,
I owe to no one neither complaints nor grudges.
Now, beginning to gain a resounding fame,
I am not at all in excitation!

27. 再次函請香港李博嵐院長 為購英漢字典

醉花陰
蓬安勞改營
1979 年 5 月 27 日

秋水望穿鴻雁杳，
三月望空抱。
何在箇中由？
李鐸他遷，
處境疑雲罩。

精神振作函重草，
實況難於道。
尺牘李親收，
賜覆郵書：
向主虔誠禱！

27. Once Again Requesting By Letter Fr. Prior Paulinus Li In Hong Kong To purchase English-Chinese Dictionaries

To the Tune of Zui Hua Yin
(Tipsy in the Flowers' Shade)
Peng'an Labor-Reform Camp
May 27, 1979

Gazing eagerly at the horizon,
I caught no sight of the swan goose, the letter.
For three months,
I cherished my expectations in vain.
What is its reason?
Fr. Paulinus may have moved to another place,
And my plight is shrouded with suspicion,

Now,
I bestir myself
To write the letter once more.
But it is very difficult for me
To tell my real situation.
I hope
That Fr. Paulinus will open the letter personally,
Send a reply,
And mail to me the books.
For this,
I pray to the Lord reverently!

28. 收到訂閱的英文版和法文版《北京周報》

烏夜啼
蓬安勞改營
1979 年 7 月 9 日

暌違法語英文，
念餘春；
《周報》今收、
重晤實歡欣。

一得便，
即瀏覽，
舊情溫。
成效如何、
計較莫斤斤。

28.   Receiving The Subscribed *Beijing Review* In English And French Editions

To the Tune of Wu Ye Ti
(Crows Cawing at Night)
Peng'an Labor-Reform Camp
July 9, 1979

I have departed from
My French and my English
For more than twenty springs.
Today,
In receiving the *Review*,
I really exult in seeing them again.

No sooner at convenience
Than I will browse through the *Review*
To revive our old friendships.
About what will be the result,
I do not haggle over every ounce.

29. 與獄吏任幹事抗辯
於召見時

滿庭芳
蓬安勞改營
1979 年 7 月 13 日

『總結嘗違，
　大評今抗，
　不知究為何因？』
『立場維護，
　信仰恪遵循。』
『信教自由早佈，
　去年裡，
　新憲重申。』
『害忠善，
　自由安在？
　體驗已多春！』

『披身，
　宗教服，
　寫文惑眾，
　犯法殃民。』

29.   Contradicting Prison Official Ren During His summoning

To the Tune of Man Ting Fang
(Fully Fragrant Court)
Peng'an Labor-Reform Camp
July 13, 1979

"Having ever violated
The summary annual appraisal,
You now defy
The great semiannual appraisal.
I wonder what is your reason for?"
"I have to uphold to my stand
And to adhere respectfully to my Faith."
"The freedom of religion
Has been announced long ago,
And was reaffirmed last year
By the new Constitution."
"Since our loyal and good faithful
Have been injured,
Where is the freedom?
I myself have alredy experienced
This injury personally
For many springs!"

"Having worn the religious clothing,
You wrote articles to mislead people;
You broke the law
And ruined the people."

『撰函道真情，
　衛**教**殷殷。』
『宗教聽憑信奉，
　能愛國，
　前景如昀。』
『忠於主，
　堅持**信仰**，
　態度表諄諄。』

"I wrote the letter
To tell the real facts
And to defend the Church ardently."
"We allow you to believe in religion;
If you can love the country,
Your vista will be
As bright as the sunlight."
"Resolute to be loyal to the Lord
And to insist on my Faith,
I express my attitude earnestly."

30. 看電影《紅日》，思張靈甫將軍

人月圓
蓬安勞改營
1979 年 7 月 14 日

將軍剿共為安邦，
奮戰魯沙場。
重圍身陷，
裹屍馬革，
百世流芳！

英姿驍勇，
犧牲壯烈，
早受稱揚。
而今電影，
是非顛倒，
貶損何傷?!

30.   Watching
The Film *The Morning Sun*
And Thinking Of
The General Zhang Lingfu

To the Tune of Ren Yue Yuan
(The Family Reunion and the Full Moon)
Peng'an Labor-Reform Camp
July 14, 1979

For bringing peace to the country,
You, General Zhang, engaged
In wiping out the Communists.
You had fought bravely
In the battlefield of Shandong.
You were bogged down
In tight encirclement,
But you preferred to battle to the end,
To die and to be wrapped in a horse's hide.
You have left a good name
For a hundred generations to come!

With a valiant bearing,
In a hero's and martyr's death,
You had been praised long ago.
The present film
Turns the truth upside down.
What injuries can reach you
From its belittling ?!

31. 大評整規無攪擾

菩薩蠻
蓬安勞改營
1979 年 8 月 1 日

驕陽六月藏威武，
大評審查悠閒度。
七月整監規，
鬥批風未吹。

北京「開放」講，
「改革」征程上。
待旦枕戈忠，
任憑狼逞凶。

31.   No Disturbance During The Midyear Great Appraisal And The Rectificatin Of The Prison Rules

To the Tune of Pusa Man
(Strange Goddess)
Peng'an Labor-Reform Camp
August 1, 1979

The scorching sun in June
Concealed its force;
The midyear great appraisal
Passed in my leisure and ease.
During the rectification of the prison rules
In July,
The wind of criticizing and struggling
Did not blow in my face.

Beijing is talking about "opening-up,"
And its "reform" is setting off.
As for me, a loyal heart,
I must be on the alert,
And wait for daybreak
With my head pillowed on my weapon.
No matter how the Wolf
Will act violently against me.

32. 鐵窗好友傅志雄 調往南充

踏莎行
蓬安勞改營
1979 年 9 月 20 日

讕陋明知，
仍來遷就，
課程英語聽傳授。
秋風瑟瑟唱驪歌，
前來告別愁眉皺。

祝願恭呈：
壯懷依舊，
英文學習持恆久。
來朝獄外苟相逢，
友情八月重回首！

32.   My Good Friend In Prison, Mr. Fu Zhixiong, Is Transferred To Nanchong

To the Tune of Ta Suo Xing
(Walking across the Meadow)
Peng'an Labor-Reform Camp
September 20, 1979

Knowing very well my English is shallow.
You still condescended to come to listen
To my teaching on the English course.
In the rustling of the autumn wind,
Singing your farewell song,
You came to take leave of me
With worried look.

I offer you my wishes with respect:
Keeping your lofty ideals as usual
And persisting in learning your English.
If some day in the future,
We meet again outside prison,
Let us look back on
Our friendship of eight months once more!

33. 鳥兒怨
（爲鐵窗好友賈啓明改寫）

五律
蓬安勞改營
1979 年 11 月 24 日

似易九霄攀，
棲身斯土難。
巢兒遭累毀，
威脅受頻繁。
覓食飛田地，
尋蟲往禿山。
日常生活苦，
好轉在何年？

33.   The Bird Complains
(Rewritten for My Good Friend in Prison, Mr. Jia Qiming)

In the Poetic Style of Wulu
Peng'an Labor-Reform Camp
November 24, 1979

Ascending the highest of heavens
Seemingly easier,
I find it difficult
To reside here in this land.
My nest suffers destruction time and again;
I am frequently threatened.
To hunt for food,
I fly to the fields;
To look for insects,
I go to barren hills.
My daily life is arduous.
In what year
Will my life improve?

34. 故事片《阿詩瑪》
觀後感

風蝶令
蓬安勞改營
1979 年 11 月 26 日

曼舞輕歌美，
阿詩彝女英。
同兄奮勇抗強橫，
雖死雖狂青史永留名！

鐐銬毆批鬥，
孤牢辱綁繩：
昔曾靠主戰而贏。
切盼北京棄暗早投明！

34. Thoughts After Watching The Feature Film *A Shima*

To the Tune of Feng Die Ling
(The Butterflies in the Winds)
Peng'an Labor-Reform Camp
November 26, 1979

The graceful dance and the light music
Are beautiful;
A Shima, a girl of Yizu, Yi nationality,
Is outstanding.
Together with her elder brother, A He,
She resists strenuously the despotic.
Despite hounded to death or to madness,
They have left their names in history forever!

Fetters, handcuffs, beatings, criticisms and struggles,
Solitary cell, insults and binding ropes:
All these I have battled and conquered
In my former days,
Relying on the Lord.
I sincerely hope that
Beijing will abandon darkness for light very soon!

35. 看電影《蔡文姬》有感

菩薩蠻
蓬安勞改營
1979 年 12 月 9 日

別兒悼父文姬痛，
還鄉再醮千情湧。
修史露才華，
悲詩如晚霞。

抗魔牢已坐，
猶可頭顱破。
衛**教**佈**真**光，
樂於酸苦嘗！

35.   Reflections
On Watching The film *Cai Wenji*

To the Tune of Pusa Man
(Strange Goddess)
Peng'an Labor-Reform Camp
December 9, 1979

Departing her sons,
Mourning over her father,
Cai Wenji was sorrowful.
Having returned to her native place
And remarried,
She felt an upsurge of countless emotions.
In writing the history,
She revealed her literary talent.
Her poems of sorrow are
As touching and beautiful as sunset glow.

To resist the Demon,
Though I have been already imprisoned,
I would still like
To have my head bashed and battered.
To defend the Church,
To spread the light of Truth,
I take delight to undergo bitterness!

36. 贈鐵窗好友賈啓明

七律
蓬安勞改營
1979 年 12 月 10 日

遠非墨客或騷人，
為主吟詩抒臆欣。
問道於盲難上路，
寡聞孤陋愧蒙恩。
文辭斟酌嘗殫思，
音韻鏗鏘亦費神。
天色當前仍晦暗，
鳴蟬猶噤況囚身！

36.   A Poem For My Good Friend In Prison, Mr. Jia Qiming

In the Poetic Style of Qilu
Peng'an Labor-Reform Camp
December 10, 1979

I am far from a writer or a poet;
I rejoice to compose my poetry for the Lord
To express my feelings.
Since you ask the way
From a blind person,
You may find it difficult
To begin your journey;
Since I am ignorant and ill-informed,
I myself feel ashamed
To accept your kindness.

To weigh your words,
I racked my brains;
To make the meter and rhymn
Melodious and sonorous,
I taxed also my energy.
At present,
In the still dark and gloomy color of the sky,
Since the cicada keeps silent as before,
Let us, with the status of prisoner,
Remain quiet as well!

37. 悼「文化大革命」

（爲鐵窗好友賈啓明改寫）

七律
蓬安勞改營
1979 年 12 月 11 日

吶喊江姚林舉纛，

「英明領袖」啟航程。

紅書《語錄》常恭讀，

指示「最高」嚴執行。

無數黎民身志喪，

大批典籍爐灰成！

何天「文革」年方十？

借問「導師」棺水晶！

37.   Mourning Over
The Great Cultural Revolution
(Rewritten for my good friend in prison, Mr. Jia Qiming)

In the Poetic Style of Qilu
Peng'an Labor-Reform Camp
December 11, 1979

With the shouting of Jiang Qing and Yao Wenyuan,
Under the big army banner raised by Lin Biao,
The "wise Leader" started his voyage.
His red book, the *Quotations*,
Was always read with reverence,
His "supreme" instructions
Were sternly carried out.
Countless people had lost
Their bodies and their ideals;
Piles of important literature
Were burnt to ashes.
For what reason
Did the Revolution die premature
At the age of ten?
We ask you, "Master",
In the crystal sarcophagus!

38. 喜讀唐詩
（為鐵窗好友賈啟明改寫）

七律
蓬安勞改營
1979 年 12 月 12 日

《唐詩三百》得初冬，
精讀數篇喜五中。
政績貞開昭若日，
詩章李杜壯如虹。
天寒地凍襟懷狹，
日麗風和詩興濃。
好景自由殷切盼，
吟風弄月暢心胸！

38.   A delight In Reading
Some Poems Of The Tang Dynasty
(Rewritten for my good friend in prison, Mr. Jia Qiming)

In the Poetic Style of Qilu
Peng'an Labor-Reform Camp
December 12, 1979

This early winter,
I got a copy of
The *Three Hundred Poems of The Tang Dynasty.*
I read several pieces intensively and thoroughly,
Feeling a great joy in my heart.
The achievements of the Zhenguan and Kaiyuan
Were as evident as the sun;
The poetry of Li Bai and Du Fu
Were as magnificent as the rainbow.
The cold weather and the frozen ground
Make our being narrow;
The bright sunshine and the gentle breeze
Deepen our poetic inspiration.
I ardently expect
A beautiful scenery and freedom
To sing the wind and the moon,
To write sentimental poems with a happy heart!

39. 辭歲主前

摸魚兒
蓬安勞改營
1979 年 12 月 31 日

夏秋初，
教宗英傑，
波蘭**山姆**曾訪。
真光傳播人心振，
千萬庶民瞻仰。
刀雪亮，
逐霸業、
頓河白鴿徒然放。
力藏兇相，
為外獲支援，
內興經濟，
「四化」**北京**望。

腸將斷，
渺渺茫茫反響，
書函嘗寄蓉港。

39. Bidding Fairwell
To The Outgoing Year
In The Presence Of The Lord

To the Tune of Mo Yu Er
(Trying to Catch Fish)
Peng'an Labor-Reform Camp
December 31, 1979

In early summer and early autumn,
The eminent Pope
Visited Poland and America respectively.
Spreading the light of Truth
And inspiring the hearts of the people,
He was looked at reverently
By ten million people.
With dazzling sword in hand,
Pursuing hegemony,
The Don vainly released white doves.
Making every effort
To hide their fierce looks,
Beijing wanted to get support abroad
And to invigorate its inside economy,
Hoping the Four Modernizations.

I am heartbroken
About receiving any responses
To my letters mailed to Chengdu and Hong Kong.

英文復習還人授，
身價神兵高漲。
評審抗，
卻未遇、
鬥批鐐銬誣毆綁。
年終憶往，
任澎湃心潮，
歡多慮少，
辭歲主前暢！

I began to review my English
And also to teach it to others;
This brought me, a Divine Soldier,
A rising up personal value.
Despite resisting the year-end appraisal,
I did not run into any adversity:
Such as to be strggled against
Or criticized or shackled or handcuffed
Or slandered or beaten or bound up.
At the end of the year,
Recalling the past,
Though upsurging of my thoughts and emotions,
Much joyful and less anxious,
I see off the old year
In the presence of the Lord,
With an ease of mind!

40. 新年祝願

點絳脣
蓬安勞改營
1980 年 1 月 1 日

赤縣長空，
雲稀風小多晴朗。
氣氛清爽，
萬眾心舒暢。

出獄回家，
去國千方想。
驪歌唱，
故園終往。
祝願呈穹蒼！

40.   My New Year Wishes

To the Tune of Dian Jiang Chun
(Rouged Lips)
Peng'an Labor-Reform Camp
January 1, 1980

In the vast sky of China, the Divine Land,
There will be
Tiny clouds, gentle winds
And many clear days.
In such clear and fresh atmosphere,
Millions of people
Will feel happy in their hearts.

I want to get out of prison
And to return home.
I will try to leave the country
By every possible means.
I hope to sing the parting song
And finally to rejoin
My old monastic community.
I present all my wishes to Heaven!

41. 新年感懷

（爲鐵窗好友賈啓明改寫）

鵲橋仙
蓬安勞改營
1980 年 1 月 3 日

「鬥爭綱領」，
束之高閣，
粉墨登場「四化」。
黎元振奮務工農；
看**赤縣**、
前程如畫。

停工休息，
佳餚享受，
電影晚間風雅。
晴空萬里尚難期；
出狴犴、
何年何夏？

41.   My New Year Thoughts
(Rewritten for my good friend in prison, Mr. Jia Qiming)

To the Tune of Que Qiao Xian
(The Magpie Bridge)
Peng'an Labor-Reform Camp
January 3, 1980

"The guiding principles of class struggle"
Are Now shelved.
The Four Modernizations
Appear and go on stage,
Gratifying the people
And Cheering them
To do their industrial and agricultural works.
Behlod!
Our country, the Divine Land,
Has a picturesque future!

Stopping to labor,
We enjoy a rest and delicious food;
We watch tranquil and elegant movies
In the evenings.
It is still hard
To expect a clear boundless sky.
To get out of prison,
Will it occur to me
In what year?
In what summer?

42. 贈鐵窗好友賈啓明

水調歌頭
蓬安勞改營
1980 年 1 月 6 日

四月過從密，
彼此五中知。
或由志趣相近，
談論屢詩詞。
只是敲門探路，
遠未升堂入室，
原本昧於詩。
俯首來求教，
愧汗濕囚衣。

讀尊作，
細斟酌，
實難批。
三思改件，
遠非合律少瑕疵。
天上烏雲仍有，
獄內寒風猶拂，
不可再毫揮。
管見由衷獻，
但願爾深思。

42.   A Poem For
My Good Friend In Prison,
Mr. Jia Qiming

To the Tune of Shui Diao Ge Tou
(The Song of the Water Music)
Peng'an Labor-Reform Camp
January 6, 1980

We have been in frequent contact for four months,
And know each other's heart.
Probably,
Owing to your aspiration and interest close to mine,
We have talked about the poetry frequently.
My poetic level is only at the stage
Of knocking at the door and finding out the way,
But not of passing through the hall into the inner chamber.
Originally,
I am ignorant of the poetry.
When you stooped to ask for advice,
My sweat perspired from shame dampened my prison garb.

Reading your writings,
I attentively considered and weighed your words.
I felt it seemingly difficult to do the revising and correcting.
Though having been pondered over and over,
My corrected pages were not totally accordant
With the poetic rules, nor less defective.
In the sky there are still dark clouds,
And in the prison the cold winds sweep as before,
You may not wield your brush any more.
I offer to you my humble opinion
From the bottom of my heart,
Hoping you to give a careful consideration.

43. 全監大會

漁歌子
蓬安勞改營
1980 年 1 月 21 日

大會今開在廣場，
整規懲騖獎馴良。
「蘿」舞動，
「棒」揮揚，
群囚俯首好還鄉。

43.   A Great Assembly
Of The Whole Prison

To the Tune of Yu Ge Zi
(Fisherman's Song)
Peng'an Labor-Reform Camp
January 21, 1980

Today,
A general meeting is held
In the open.
It aimed at
Rectifying the prison rules,
Punishing the unyielding and disobeying,
And rewarding the tame and docile.
Attracted by the waving "carrot",
And frightened by the "stick",
All the prisoners bow their heads
So that they may return
To their native places.

44. 喜迎春節

（為鐵窗好友賈啟明改寫）

春光好
蓬安勞改營
1980 年 2 月 16 日

「主席」逝，
「四人」囚，
變神州。
感覺和風響颼颼，
喜心頭。

「四化」藍圖壯麗，
合乎萬眾期求。
長陷監牢離去望，
豈今秋？

44. Joyously Welcoming
The Spring Festival
(Rewritten for my good friend in prison, Mr. Jia Qiming)

To the Tune of Chun Guang Hao
(The Beautiful Spring Light)
Peng'an Labor-Reform Camp
February 16, 1980

The death of the "President"
And the imprisonment of the "Four People"
Brought change to the Divine Land.
Feeling the gentle breeze
Blowing and rustling,
I am cheerful in my heart.

The splendid blueprint
For the "Four Modernizations"
Accords with
The expectations and desires
Of millions of prople.
Having been put in prison for a long time,
I wish, I hope to get out.
In this autumn will it be?

45. 劉少奇近獲平反昭雪
（為鐵窗好友賈啓明改寫）

桂殿秋
蓬安勞改營
1980 年 3 月 3 日

毛忌恨，

儘頭低，

劉仍受虐死悽悽。

喪生「文革」究多少？

禍首晶棺或略知！

45.   Liu Shaoqi Recently Obtains His Redress And Rehabilitation
(Rewritten for my good friend in prison, Mr. Jia Qiming)

To the Tune of Gui Dian Qiu
(Antumn in the Cassia Hall)
Peng'an Labor-Reform Camp
March 3, 1980

Hated by Mao,
Though already bowed his head,
Liu was still tyrannized so cruelly
As to his mournful death.
How many prople lost their lives
During the Great Cultural Revolution?
The chief culprit
In the crystal sarcophagus
Must probably have a rough idea!

46. 獄友任雲開
挨鬥一月終乞降

采桑子
蓬安勞改營
1980 年 3 月 17 日

會中一月遭批鬥，
任犯心傷。
難再頑強，
終得低頭而請降！

折磨囚犯心身志，
赤獄猖狂。
鐵幕淒涼，
究到何時方喪亡?!

46.   Fellow Prisoner, Mr. Ren Yunkai, Surrenders Eventually After Being Struggled For One Month

To the Tune of Cai Sang Zi
(Picking Mulberries)
Peng'an Labor-Reform Camp
March 17, 1980

Criticized and struggled in meetings
For one month,
Prisoner Ren is sorrowful in heart.
He cannot remain tenacious.
He has ultimately no choice
But to hang his head and to surrender.

Tormenting prisoners' minds, bodies
Wills, spirits and ideals,
The Red prison is savage.
The Iron Curtain is bleak.
Until what time
Will it pass after all ?!

47. 悼薩爾瓦多總主教羅梅羅

洞仙歌
蓬安勞改營
1980 年 4 月 4 日

和平維護，
卓著公勳績。
諾獎榮膺令名熠。
眾魔憎，
遇刺身殞歸**天**；
十萬人，
送葬祝公安息！

人民多信**主**，
興旺工農，
祖國原當享安謐。
共黨竟掀風，
政客爭權；
時局穩，
談何容易！
公殉難**天堂**定榮登！
望世界和平，
主前求錫！

47. Grieving Over His Excellency Romero, Archbishop Of El Salvador

To the Tune of Dong Xian Ge
(The Song of the Fairies in the Grotto)
Peng'an Labor-Reform Camp
April 4, 1980

In Maintaining the peace,
Your Excellency, Archbishop,
Your meritorious exploits were outstanding.
You were once honored with the Nobel Prize for Peace
And enjoyed a brilliant reputation.
Hated by demons,
You suffered assassination, died and returned to God.
A hundred thousand people attended your funeral,
Wishing you rest in peace!

Most of the Salvadorians believe in the Lord,
And the industry and the agriculture are flourishing.
Your homeland must originally enjoy the tranquility.
Yet,
The Communists have raised the wind,
And politicians scramble for power;
It is not easy to get the current situation stable!
Since,
Having died a martyr,
You must surely have ascended gloriously to Heaven!
We wish:
You will plead for world peace
In the presence of the Lord!

48. 全營假釋大會

鵲橋仙
蓬安勞改營
1980 年 4 月 7 日

訊聞數日；
囚凡念載，
假釋特恩即沐。
今朝大會廣場開，
十五犯、
蒙恩出獄。

吾將獲釋；
謠傳會後，
熄滅如窗前燭。
監牢長坐恨全無，
卻只願、
忠於基督！

48.   A Great Meeting Of The Whole Camp For The Release On Parole

To the Tune of Que Qiao Xian
(The Magpie Bridge)
Peng'an Labor-Reform Camp
April 7, 1980

I have heard for several days the news:
A prisoner who has been imprisoned for twenty years
Will receive a special favor-release on parole.
Today,
A great assembly is held in the square;
Fifteen prisoners have been given
This favor of being released from prison.

Concerning my impending release
The rumor now goes out after the assembly,
As the candle outside the window extinguishing.
For my part,
I have no grudge at all
Of being so long put behind bars.
My only wish is to be faithful to Christ!

49. 看電影《傲蕾一蘭》有懷

洞仙歌
蓬安勞改營
1980 年 4 月 7 日

為民為父，
抗敵成俘願。
鐵鏈牢中作常伴；
七年堅，
逃返見疑於人。
重披掛，
勝敵榮歸眾讚。

湧狂風駭浪，
震撼漁船，
悲憤填膺起迎戰。
挨鬥復遭關，
判處長刑；
綁鐐銬，
辱批毆譴。
茹苦念餘年首仍昂；
依靠主神通，
凱旋弦箭！

49.   Reflections
On Watcing The Film *Ao Lei Yi Lan*

To the Tune of Dong Xian Ge
(The Song of the Fairies in the Grotto)
Peng'an Labor-Reform Camp
April 7, 1980

For his people and his father,
She, Ao Lei, Was ready and glad
To become a captive in resisting the enemy.
The iron chain was her eternal companion in prison;
She was firm and unbending for seven years.
She finally escaped, returned home,
But was suspected.
She buckled on her armor;
She overcame the enemy.
Returning gloriously,
She was praised by all.

When violent winds and fierce waves were raised,
The Fishing Boat was shocked.
Filled with grief and indignation,
I arose to meet head-on.
I was struggled against and then imprisoned.
Condemned to long-term sentence,
I was to suffer from
Being bound or shackled or handcuffed
Or insulted or criticized or beaten or reproached.
Having endured hardships for over 20 years,
I hold my head high as always.
Depending on the immense might of the Lord,
My triumph is like an arrow on the string!

50. 贈鐵窗好友周邦舊
（爲鐵窗好友賈啓明改寫）

七律
蓬安勞改營
1980 年 4 月 27 日

鐵骨錚錚目擊難，
今朝勞改遇君歡。
有緣相識於囹圄，
無懼交談示寸丹。
興趣濃濃詩試賦，
熱情滿滿稿糾刪。
料君很快將離去，
風貌恩情骨永鐫！

50.   For Mr. Zhou Bangjiu, A Good Friend In Prison

(Rewritten for my good friend in prison, Mr. Jia Qiming)

In the Poetic Style of Qilu
Peng'an Labor-Reform Camp
April 27, 1980

It was difficult
To see with my own eyes
A person, staunch and unyielding.
Now,
During the period of my labor-reform,
I was very joyful
To meet you, such as this outstanding man.
I have a destiny
To be acquainted with you in jail;
I was not afraid
To talk with you and to show you my heart.
With a deep interest,
I wonld like to compose my poems;
You have done
The corrections and revisions on my drafts,
With fully warm feelings.
I think
That you will depart very soon.
Yct,
Your appearance, bearing and kindness
Will be engraved on my bones forever!

51. 關於
「劉少奇同志追悼大會」

踏莎行
蓬安勞改營
1980 年 5 月 21 日

權位毛專，

劉遭憎惡，

獄中慘死十寒暑。

叛徒工賊內奸成，

下場主席何淒楚！

悼會今開，

追懷安撫；

冤魂瞑目能陰府?!

隱藏毛惡或當然

皮亡中共將焉附?!

51.   Concerning "The Memorial Meeting Of Comrade Liu Shaoqi"

To the Tune of Ta Suo Xing
(Walking across the Meadow)
Peng'an Labor-Reform Camp
May 21, 1980

Mao monopolized power and position.
Liu was hated by him
And died a tragic death in prison
Ten winters and summers ago.
He was leveled on
As a traitor, scab and enemy agent.
How sorrowful was his end,
The end of the "head of State"!

Now,
A mourning meeting is held
For his remembrance,
For his consolation.
Can this bring the wronged person's ghost
To close his eyes in the netherworld ?!
It may be only natural
To cover up the evil of Mao,
Their "Great Leader" and their skin!
Otherwise,
The Chinese Communist Party,
Their great part and their hair,
What will it adhere to ?!

52. 欣悉
郎毓秀教授近況於報章

菩薩蠻
蓬安勞改營
1980 年 8 月 5 日

報章最近傳音訊，
年逾花甲仍風韻。
「文革」禍殃完，
返回原講壇。

封喉停教苦，
強忍十寒暑。
祝願暢心身，
尤望蒙主恩！

52.   Learning Gladly From The Newspaper The Current Situation Of Professor Pansy Lang Yuxiu

To the Tune of Pusa Man
(Strange Goddess)
Peng'an Labor-Reform Camp
August 5, 1980

The newspaper recently delivered a news:
That you, Professor Pansy Lang,
Though over sixty,
Remained still charming.
When the disaster of the Cultural Revolution
Was approaching to its end,
You returned to your original platform.

The suffering from sealing up your throat
And from stopping your teaching,
You managed to endure
For ten winters and summers.
I wish that
You will always be happy in mind and in body,
And, particularly, that
You will always receive favors from the Lord!

53. 獎金頒又撤

清平樂
蓬安勞改營
1980 年 8 月 21 日

獎金蒙贈，
受賞囚高興。
超過三元額外領，
幹活自當拼命。

閥門質劣銷難，
庫房積壓如山。
頒獎兩遭即止，
合情合理當然！

53. Money Award,
To Be Issued, But Soon Canceled

To the Tune of Qing Ping Yue
(The Qing Ping Song)
Peng'an Labor-Reform Camp
August 21, 1980

Awarded
With a money bonus and a reward,
The prisoners were cheerful.
Having received an extra three dollars,
Each one of them would certainly exert
His utmost to do the labor.

Owing to the low quality,
The valves, their products,
Have no markets,
And have been overstocked
In the storehouse
So much as piling up like a hill.
The award, ever issued twice,
Should be stopped right now.
This ought to be fair and reasonable!

54. 年中大評無挑戰

點絳脣
蓬安勞改營
1980 年 9 月 1 日

恐怖氛圍，
大評三月籠囚犯。
鬥爭批判，
喧嚷沖霄漢。

面對**神兵**，
見一仍舊貫；
難挑戰，
網開一面，
彼此均方便！

54.   No Challenge From The Midyear Appraisal

To the Tune of Dian Jiang Chun
(Rouged Lips)
Peng'an Labor-Reform Camp
September 1, 1980

The terrific atmosphere shrouded the prisoners
During three months of the midyear appraisal.
From the struggling and the criticizing,
The clamor, roars and shouts
Resounded to the skies.

Facing me, a Divine Warrior,
They saw me acting as before.
Thinking it difficult
To challenge me to battle,
They left to me one side of the net open,
So that we, they and I, all
Are feeling suitable!

55. 道德教育

定風波
蓬安勞改營
1980 年 9 月 6 日

結束大評剛五天，
今開大會又全監。
政委宣稱施德教，
強調，
於囚改造實攸關。

運動時長聲勢壯，
喧嚷，
除舊更新思行言。
改造強行跟**黨**走，
能否？
江山**中共**百千年？

55. **Education In Ethics**

To the Tune of Ding Feng Bo
(Calming Storm)
Peng'an Labor-Reform Camp
September 6, 1980

Just on the fifth day
After the close of the great appraisal,
An assembly of the whole prison
Is today convened once more.
The Regiment Political Commissar
Professed a moral education to be carried out,
Emphasizing that this would be
With the prisoners' reformation at stake.

He said that the campaign would be
Long in time and giganstic in scale.
He clamored that we should do away
With the old of our thoughts, deeds and words
And usher them in the new.
If we all are forced to be reformed
And to follow the Party's heels,
Will it be possible
That the state power of the Chinese Communists
Will endure one or ten hundred years?

56. 獄中國慶

漁歌子
蓬安勞改營
1980 年 10 月 1 日

享用佳餚沐日光，
坐看電影聽唱腔。
風拂面，
耳聞傷，
哀鳴出自小監房！

56.   National Day In Prison

To the Tune of Yu Ge Zi
(Fisherman's Song)
Peng'an Labor-Reform Camp
October 1, 1980

We enjoy the delicious food,
We are bathed in the sunlight.
We sit and watch a movie,
Listening to the Chinese melodies.
When breeze caresses my face,
My ears hear sorrowfully
A plaintive weep and wail
Coming from a solitary cell!

57. 獲四兄回信

如夢令
蓬安勞改營
1980 年 10 月 17 日

致信四兄新近，
今獲回函興奮。
現狀讓粗知，
來日遷居欣允。
欣允，
欣允，
謝主促兄紓困。

57.   Receiving A Reply
From My Fourth-Elder Brother

To the Tune of Ru Meng Ling
(Like a Dream)
Peng'an Labor-Reform Camp
October 17, 1980

Recently,
I wrote to my fourth-elder brother.
Today,
I obtain a reply from him
With excitement.
He let me have a rough idea
Of his current situation;
He gladly consented to my moving there
To live with him some day in the future.
Gladly consented,
Gladly consented,
I am grateful to the Lord
For urging him
To free me from my difficult position.

58. 陪王明雪幹事趕場

菩薩蠻
蓬安勞改營
1980 年 10 月 27 日

縣城趕集買煙葉，
叫同前往王明雪。
出獄即忠貞，
好心王表明。

人流洶似浪，
集市供銷旺。
盛況見而歡，
謝忱呈昊天。

58.   Accompanying Official Wang Mingxue To Go To The Market

To the Tune of Pusa Man
(Strange Goddess)
Peng'an Labor-Reform Camp
October 27, 1980

To go to the market in the county town
To buy tobacco,
Official Wang Mingxue asked me
To accompany him.
Knowing that I, a loyal Cathobic,
Might leave the prison very soon,
He would like
To make known to me his kind heart.

In the fair there was a stream of people,
Surging as raging waves.
The market was very exuberant
Both in supplying and in marketing.
I took delight
In witnessing this spectacular affair,
And I offered my gratitude to Heaven.

59. 拒守新樓房

七律
蓬安勞改營
1980 年 11 月 12 日

新房本隊建河濱，
看守夜間需四人。
令接忠心堅拒絕，
命承餘犯立遵循。
熬磨寒夜難贏體，
欲閱英刊實主因。
幹事聞音無責怪，
成功抗命謝天恩。

59. Refusing To Watch The New Building

In the Poetic Style of Qilu
Peng'an Labor-Reform Camp
November 12, 1980

Our company has been constructing
A new building along a small river.
Four people are needed
To keep guard all night.
On receiving the order,
I, a loyal Catholic, rejected firmly to obey;
Yet, for the rest of the prisoners,
No sooner had they received the command
Than complied immediately.
My thin and weak body
Is unable to stay up late all the cold night;
But the primary reason really is
That I want
To read the English publication at night.
On hearing this news from me,
The official did not reproach me.
I was appreciative to the favor of Heaven
For having succeeded in defying their order.

60. 致比利時母院信面
被營部退回

浣溪沙
蓬安勞改營
1980 年 11 月 29 日

致李信函昨退回，
港郵標示李遷離，
七週期望化為灰。

母院西歐今去信，
發還營部感悲悽，
只緣去國失良機。

60.   My Letter To The Mother Abbey In Belgium Returned By The Camp Authorities

To the Tune of Huan Xi Sha
(Yarn Washed in the Stream)
Peng'an Labor-Reform Camp
November 29, 1980

My letter to Fr. Prior Paulinus Li
Was returned yesterday.
The Hong Kong post office
Marked with Li's moving out.
My expectation of seven weeks
Turns to ashes.

Today,
I have written
To my mother abbey in West Europe.
But the camp authorities
Gave the letter back to me.
This made me sad,
For a golden opportunity
Of my leaving the country slipped!

61. 為鐵窗友人蘭光友
寫申訴

生查子
蓬安勞改營
1980 年 12 月 3 日

故鄉權勢憎，
蘭乃他方去。
行竊入監牢，
十載長刑處。

為人寫獄中，
唯一斯申訴。
多犯久含冤，
盡雪何寒暑?!

61.   Writing An Apeal For Mr. Lan Guangyou, A Friend In Prison

To the Tune of Sheng Zha Zi
(Fresh Berries)
Peng'an Labor-Reform Camp
December 3, 1980

Hated by the power in his native place,
Lan had to go to alien land.
He was put in jail for theft
And sentenced to ten years, a long term.

I have written for people in prison
Only this appeal.
Many prisoners have long suffered
Injustices.
In what winter and summer
Will they all be exonerated ?!

62. 夜讀燈下

清平樂
蓬安勞改營
1980 年 12 月 11 日

電燈高掛，
稍遠離床架。
晝做苦工無空暇，
夜讀只能燈下。

英文法語重溫，
輕微收效一春。
視力損傷燈暗，
心中湧現愁雲。

62.   Reading At Night By Lamplight

To the Tune of Qing Ping Yue
(The Qing Ping Song)
Peng'an Labor-Reform Camp
December 11, 1980

The electric light hangs
High and a little distant from my bed.
In the daytime,
When I have to do hard labor,
I have no free time;
I can only read
At night by lamplight.

In reviewing my English and my French,
The effect for a year is slight.
Owing to that the light is dim,
My eyesight is damaged;
Gloomy clouds arise in my heart.

63. 向蓬安縣人民法院
再遞申訴

卜算子
蓬安勞改營
1980 年 12 月 18 日

七十五天前，
法院交申訴。
平反回音卻渺然，
究為何緣故？

申訴現重提，
切盼糾差錯。
縱使期望全落空，
絕不將頭俯。

63.   Submitting My Appeal Once Again To The Peng'an County People's Court

To the Tune of Pu Suan Zi
(The Fortune Teller)
Peng'an Labor-Reform Camp
December 18, 1980

Seventy-five days ago,
I submitted my appeal
To the court.
But the reply for rehabilitation
Is remote and dim.
What is its reason?

Now,
I hand over my appeal once again,
Eagerly looking forward to redressing the wrong.
Even if my expectations
Come to naught entirely,
I will never bow my head.

64. 聽到王明雪幹事
在中隊會上
關於我拒寫年終總結的
驚人的講話

人月圓
蓬安勞改營
1980 年 12 月 31 日

「年終總結眾須寫，
　抗命僅一人。
　容周有故：
『自由信教，』
　新憲重申。」

「效尤如有，
　嚴懲不貸；
　告誡諄諄。」
　王言入耳，
　主恩深謝，
　鶴立雞群！

64.   Hearing The Surprising Remarks By Official Wang Mingxue At The Company Meeting Concerning My Refusal To Write My Year-End Summary

To the Tune of Ren Yue Yuan
(The Family Reunion and the Full Moon)
Peng'an Labor-Reform Camp
December 31, 1980

"All of you must write
Your year-end summary.
The disobedient is only one person.
For tolerating Zhou to act independently,
There is a reason:
'Freedom of religion,'
Which our new constitution
Has just reaffirmed."

"If someone wants to follow this bad example,
He will be severely punished without mercy.
I enjoin you all assiduously."
When Wang's remarks enter my ears,
I thank deeply the Lord's blessing,
For He has made me
Like a crane standing among chickens!

65. 向耶穌辭歲

踏莎行
蓬安勞改營
1980 年 12 月 31 日

申訴提交，
全由吏勸，
撤銷但願加刑案。
粗通英語又教人，
寒酸處境徐徐暖。

詩詞吟詠，
胸懷舒展，
改詩為友憂常伴。
全年回顧滿歡欣，
耶穌慈愛深銘感！

65.   Saying Goodbye To The Outgoing Year In The Presence Of Jesus

To the Tune of Ta Suo Xing
(Walking across the Meadow)
Peng'an Labor-Reform Camp
December 31, 1980

I submitted my appeal,
Because of the advice of an official.
I wish that my case
Of the additional sentence will be rescinded.
I know a little English
And now teach it to others.
On grounds of this,
My cold situation is gradually getting warm.

From composing my poems,
I had ease of mind.
In correcting the poems of a friend,
I was always accompanied with worries.
In looking back the whole year,
I am full of joy
And deeply grateful to You, Jesus,
For Your loving-kindness!

66. 致李博嵐院長信原封退回

采桑子
蓬安勞改營
1981 年 1 月 17 日

突歸去雁何緣故？
歸自香江。
歸自香江，
李鐸而今在哪方？

失之交臂離鄉願，
百結愁腸。
百結愁腸，
後事完全交上蒼！

66.   The Letter
To Fr. Prior Paulinus Li Returned

To the Tune of Cai Sang Zi
(Picking Mulberries)
Peng'an Labor-Reform Camp
January 17, 1980

Why Should the parting goose
Suddenly come back?
It returns from Hong Kong.
It returns from Hong Kong,
Where is Fr. Paulinus now?

Having missed the golden opportunity
Of leaving my native land,
My heart is weighed down
With anxiety.
My heart is weighed down
With anxiety,
I want to utterly entrust to Heaven
What will happen to me!

67. 希臘阿陀斯山 東正教修院

鵲橋仙
蓬安勞改營
1981 年 1 月 22 日

崇高理想，
迷人景色，
蕞爾國邦豪壯。
敬神幹活度年歡，
的確是、
人間天上！

妖言今泛，
罪波遍湧
世外桃源清爽。
黑牢鐵幕陷多年，
知勝景、
心馳神往！

67.   An Orthodox Monastery On Mount Athos In Greece

To the Tune of Que Qiao Xian
(The Magpie Bridge)
Peng'an Labor-Reform Camp
January 22, 1981

With a sublime ideal,
With enchanting scenery,
The pretty State is magnificent.
Worshiping God,
Engaging in labor,
You, monks, spend your years in joy.
Truly,
You are on earth as if in Heaven!

In these days
When fallacies overflow,
When waves of sin surge,
Your haven, a tranquil place, is refreshing.
I have been involved over years
In the dark jail and behind the Iron Curtain;
Learning of your wonderful scene,
I long for you
And my thoughts fly to you!

68. 「四人幫」定罪判刑

破陣子
蓬安勞改營
1981 年 1 月 25 日

十載榮當桀犬，
欺人害世瘋狂。
毛死坐牢遭判處，
兇焰風光悉喪亡。
悽然今下場！

眾醜原形畢露，
黨中內幕張揚。
奪利爭權從未已，
長夜漫漫黎庶傷，
何時見曙光？

註：中共將王洪文、張春橋、江青和姚文元
稱作「四人幫」。

68.   "The Gang Of Four" Convicted And Sentenced

To the Tune of Po Zheng Zi
(Storming the Enemy's Position)
Peng'an Labor-Reform Camp
January 25, 1981

Honored to serve as the tyrant's curs
For ten years,
You were insane
To bully and to harm the people.
After Mao's death,
You were imprisoned and sentenced;
Both your ferocity and arrogance
Have passed and gone for ever.
How sad your end is today!

All of you, clowns, have shown your true colors;
Some inside stories of your Party
Have also been made public.
The scramble for power and profit
Among your party members has never ceased.
Living in the endless night,
The people are laden with grief.
When will they see the light of morning?

Note: The Chinese Communist Party call Wang Hongwen,
      Zhang Chunqiao, Jiang Qing and Yao Wenyuan "The
      Gang of Four."

69. 王明雪幹事退回
第二次寄香港李博嵐院長信
並予解釋

七絕
蓬安勞改營
1981 年 1 月 27 日

「寄港信函恕退還，
　新頒禁令是由緣。
　未來何必多憂慮，
　冤案撤銷定力援。」

69. Official Wang Mingxue Returns My Second Letter To Fr. Prior Paulinus Li of Hong Kong With Some Explanations

In the Poetic Style of Qijue
Peng'an Labor-Reform Camp
January 27, 1981

"Please excuse me
For returning your letter to Hong Kong!
The reson is —
A new ban has been issued recently.
No need to worry so much
Over your future!
Be assured of my support
Of reversing your unjust verdict."

70. 張犯死工地

五絕
蓬安勞改營
1981 年 2 月 1 日

八層鷹架上，
張犯墜身亡。
三日停工學，
豈真狼愛羊？

70.   Prisoner Zhang Dies In The Construction Site

In the Poetic Style of Wujue
Peng'an Labor-Reform Camp
February 1, 1981

From the eight-storey scaffolding
Prisoner Zhang fell and died.
Because of this,
We were ordered
To stop work
And hold meetings
To study for three days.
Can this show
The tender affection of the Wolf
For the sheep?

71. 春節

春光好
蓬安勞改營
1981 年 2 月 5 日

鐵窗犯，
喜洋洋，
慶春光。
歌影球棋戲雙簧，
悉登場！

活似升平景象，
真如世上**天堂**！
突兀穹蒼晴轉晦，
或堪傷！

71.　The Spring Festival

To the Tune of Chun Guang Hao
(The Beautiful Spring Light)
Peng'an Labor-Reform Camp
February 5, 1981

Prisoners behind bars rejoice
In celebrating the spring light.
Songs, movies, balls, Chinese chess,
Dramas and two-man comic shows:
All come together on stage!

This scene resembles peaceful surrounds,
Really like an earthly paradise!
Unexpectedly,
The sky changes from sunny to gloomy.
This may be rated as sorrowful!

72. 影片《賀龍元帥》
觀後感

獻衷心
蓬安勞改營
1981 年 2 月 17 日

禍殃罹「文革」,
憂憤填膺。
批鬥會,
表忠誠,
俯首聆申討,
仍繫秦城。
身心苦,
三載受,
卒於囹。

皇后恨,
暴君憎,
有功元帥裂身名。
製片申冤案,
安撫亡靈!
追根底,
翁醉意:
黨英明!

72.   Impressions After Watching The Film *Marshal He Long*

To the Tune of Xian Zhong Xin
(Presenting the Heart)
Peng'an Labor-Reform Camp
February 17, 1981

During the Cultural Revolution,
Meeting with the disaster
You, Marshal, were full of worries and indignation.
In criticism and struggle meetings,
You showed your loyalty
And bowed your head to listen to denunciations;
Yet you were still imprisoned in Qin Cheng
All the same.
Suffering in body and mind for three years,
You died in the jail.

Hated by Jiang Qing, the Queen,
And by Mao Zedong, the Tyrant,
You, a meritorious Marshal,
Lost all your standing and reputation.
To redress an injustice,
To comfort you,
Now a ghost and a soul,
A movie was produced!
To get to the root of the matter,
The drinker's heart was not in the cup,
But in demonstrating
How wise and how good the Party is!

73. 向法院遞交
第三次申訴書

浪淘沙
蓬安勞改營
1981 年 3 月 8 日

法院久拖延，
錯案糾難。
兩回申訴豈徒然？
科長週前緣故告，
義憤膺填。

振筆斥讕言，
再示貞堅，
情豪志壯字三千。
為主坐穿牢底願，
絕不腰彎！

73.   The Third Appeal To The Court

To the Tune of Lang Tao Sha
(Wave-Washed Sands)
Peng'an Labor-Reform Camp
March 8, 1981

Because of the Court's long delay,
My misjudged case is difficult to crrect.
Have my last two appeals been to no avail?
A week ago,
When the section chief told me
The reason for the delay
I was filled with righteous indignation.

I wielded my pen to upbraid the slanders,
Showing my loyalty once more.
The three thousand words express
My high ideals and my fervent sentiments.
I prefer to sit in the jail cell for the Lord
Until its bottom breaks
Than to bend down!

74. 郎毓秀教授
告別音樂會

虞美人
蓬安勞改營
1981 年 3 月 28 日

舞臺卅載長登上，
告別忘情唱。
歌聲婉轉入長空，
迴蕩昆渝京滬漢津蓉。

初期上主難歌頌，
天變隨波湧。
為君懇切禱牢房：
來日升天歌唱主慈祥！

74.   Professor Pansy Lang Yuxiu's Farewell Concerts

To the Tune of Yu Mei Ren
(The Beauty of Yu)
Peng'an Labor-Reform Camp
March 28, 1981

To the music stage
Where you have been
For as long as forty years,
Now, you say goodbye with your lusty singing.
Your sweet voice floats to the vast sky,
Reverberating all over
Kunming, Chongqing, Beijing, Shanghai,
Wuhan, Tianjin and Chengdu.

During the earlier period
You sang rarely the praises of the Lord.
When the sky changed,
You were forced to drift with the tide.
I want to pray for you in prison:
Some day you will go to Heaven
To sing the mercy of the Lord!

75. 全營總評
獎懲大會

風蝶令
蓬安勞改營
1981 年 3 月 30 日

檢查年終寫，
忠心拒絕堅。
「鬥批垢辱」未來纏，
四月會中默禱賦詩篇。

總結莊嚴會，
營方獎懲頒。
平安無事度難關，
受惠蒙恩舉首謝蒼天！

75.   An Overall Appraisal Assembly Of The Entire Camp For Rewards And Penalties

To the Tune of Feng Die Ling
(The Butterflies in the Winds)
Peng'an Labor-Reform Camp
March 30, 1981

To write my year-end self-criticism,
I, a loyal Catholic, have resolutely refused.
"Struggle, criticism, humiliations and insults"
Did not come to pester me;
During the meetings of those past four months,
I engaged in silently praying and composing new poems.

In the solemn summing-up assembly,
The camp authorities promulgated
The rewards and penalties.
Crossing over the barrier
Safely and without any trouble,
I lift up my head to thank Heaven
For His favor,
For His kindness!

76. 為鐵窗好友賈啟明
改詩有感

水調歌頭
蓬安勞改營
1981 年 4 月 2 日

十億近人口，
年歲越三千；
文明古國風采，
英俊復翩翩。
血雨腥風吹打，
花葉泥沙飛舞：
卅載變容顏。
觸景君憂憤，
宣洩以詩篇！

除強暴，
揭竿起，
係從前。
當今形勢，
驅狼逐虎遠為難。
思想身心遭壓，
基本人權被奪：
黎庶茹辛酸。
「厄運何時了？」
騷首問蒼天。

76.   Thoghts on Correcting The Poems Of My Good Friend In Prison, Mr. Jia Qining

To the Tune of Shui Diao Ge Tou
(The Song of the Water Music)
Peng'an Labor-Reform Camp
April 2, 1981

With a population close to a billion,
With a history over three thousand years,
Our ancient civilized nation has
A graceful, elegant and brilliant bearing.
In the blood of rains.
In the foul wind
Flowers, leaves, dust and sands fly and dance;
The face of the country has been changing
For thirty years.
The sight strikes worry and indignation
Into your heart
And you unbosom yourself in poems!

To get rid of the brute force,
The people raised a standard of justice:
This was in the past time.
In the current situation
It is much more difficult
To drive out the Wolf and the Tiger.
Thoughts, bodies and minds are oppressed,
The basic human rights are taken away:
The people suffer all kinds of hardships.
"When will their misfortunes come to an end?"
We may scratch our heads
And appeal to Heaven!

77. 教宗若望保祿二世
遇刺受傷

蝶戀花
蓬安勞改營
1981 年 5 月 28 日

晤眾週三遭暗算，
遇襲槍傷赤犯腸將斷！
早復安康遙祝願，
人靈多救功多建！

接見信徒常誨勉，
出訪諸邦濟世宏圖展。
冥府之門徒搗亂，
牧人豪氣衝霄漢！

77.   Pope John Paul II Shot And Wounded

To the Tune of Die Lian Hua
(Butterflies Courting Flowers)
Peng'an Labor-Reform Camp
May 28, 1981

During the Wednesday General Andience,
You, our Holy Father, fell a prey to a plot,
And you were shot and wounded.
I, a red prisoner, was heartbroken!
From afar I wish your recovery very soon
So that you may make more contributions
In redeeming more souls!

In your audience with the faithful,
You always give your instructions and encouragement.
By paying visits to some countries and nations,
You have carried out
Your great plan of savng the world.
The gates of the underworld
Have vainly attempted to create disturbance;
The noble and heroic spirit of the shepherd
Soars to the sky!

78. 宋慶齡女士病故

長相思
蓬安勞改營
1981 年 6 月 6 日

「國母」尊，
毛共跟，
厚祿高官三十春。
殃民助「暴君」！

住京申，
宅美輪，
監視常遭心似焚。
含悲了此身！

78.   Madame Song Qingling Dies From Disease

To the Tune of Chang Xiang Si
(Enduring Love)
Peng'an Labor-Reform Camp
June 6, 1981

You were called "mother of the country."
You followed Mao's Communist Party.
You enjoyed
A high position and a handsome salary
For thirty springs.
You have helped the Tyrant
To ruin the people!

You lived in Beijing and in Shanghai
In large and elegant mansions.
Always watched,
You were burning with anxiety.
With sorrow in spirit
Your life has ended!

79. 鄧以明主教
被教宗若望保祿二世
任命爲廣州總主教

江城子
蓬安勞改營
1981 年 6 月 26 日

卅年衛**教**苦酸嘗。
在座堂,
在班房,
不屈不撓奮勇戰**豺狼**。
勝利出牢於去歲,
旋治病,
赴**香江**。

月初**聖父**謁**梵岡**。
訴衷腸,
沐春光;
重任榮膺卻使**北京**惶。
放下屠刀休吼叫,
狼莫懼,
可成羊!

79.   Bishop Dominic Deng Yiming Is Appointed By Pope John Paul II Archbishop of Guangzhou

To the Tune of Jiang Cheng Zi
(The Town by the River)
Peng'an Labor-Reform Camp
June 26, 1981

In defense of the Church,
You have tasted sufferings for thirty years.
In the cathedral
And in the prison
You fought the Wolf bravely
With an unflagging spirit.
Last year you victoriously left the jail;
To cure your sickness,
You then went to Hong Kong.

Early this month
You had an audience with the Holy Father in the Vatican,
Pouring out your heart,
Bathig in the spring light.
You have just received gloriously
A post of great responsibility.
But this has brought Beijing to fear.
Please, O Beijing, do not roar,
You may lay down your butcher's knife!
You, Wolf, do not be terrified,
You can become a sheep!

80. 駁斥獄友陳錦江

水調歌頭
蓬安勞改營
1981 年 7 月 3 日

「**教會**有誰信？
何處鬼神逢？
惡勞好逸神父，
領俸悉卑躬。
任命居然主教，
內政蠻橫干涉，
真善豈**梵宮**？
爾已苦嘗夠，
何以緊跟從？」

總主教，
獲任命，
鄧公雄。
多年繫獄，
操守完好父推崇。
事件報登**陳**悉
采石場中聞諮，
當面斥**貞忠**
檢舉任憑寫，
挺立自**蒼松**！

80.   Refuting Fellow Prisoner, Chen Jinjiang

To the Tune of Shui Diao Ge Tou
(The Song of the Water Music)
Peng'an Labor-Reform Camp
July 3, 1981

"Who believes in the Church?
Where can one meet ghosts and spirits?
The priests love ease and hate work;
They all stooped down to get their official salaries.
Presuming to appoint bishop,
Interfering arbitrarily in China's internal affairs,
The Vatican, can it really be good?
As for you,
Who have tasted the bitterness to the full,
Why are you still following it so closely?"

Appointed archbishop,
Bishop Dominic Deng is heroic and great.
Jailed for many years,
He is highly praised by the Holy Father
For his integrity is still intact.
Chen learns this matter published in the newspaper;
When I heard in the quarry his calumnies,
I, a loyal Catholic, refuted him
To his face on the spot.
Whatever accusation he may write,
I, a green pine, stand upright here always!

81. 自王明雪幹事收到
法院宣佈釋放的新判決書

蝶戀花
蓬安勞改營
1981 年 7 月 22 日

晚會開完王召喚，
撤去加刑新判高聲唸。
獲釋文書糧食券，
川資津貼交當面。

歲月悠悠囚狴犴，
百戰妖魔膽赤身心健。
謝主凱歌哼婉轉，
歌聲冉冉飛霄漢。

81. Receiving From Official Wang Mingxue The New Court Verdict Declaring My Release

To the Tune of Die Lian Hua
(Butterflies Courting Flowers)
Peng'an Labor-Reform Camp
July 22, 1981

At the conclusion of the evening company assembly,
Official Wang called me to himself.
He read loudly to me the new verdict
Rescinding the original increase of my penalty.
He handed me face to face
The document declaring my release,
Grain coupons, traveling expenses and allowance.

I have been confined in jail
For long years,
For a month of Sundays.
Having fought a hundred battles against the devil.
I am still faithful to my allegiance
And healthy in body and in mind.
To thank the Lord,
I hum pleasantly and mildly
A song of triumph;
And the sound of singing
Flies slowly to the sky.

82. 回遂寧

喜春來
四川遂寧
1981 年 7 月 27 日

卅年別夢如川逝，
半百征夫勝利歸。
家鄉戰局了無知。
求**聖子**：
讓我早**西**飛！

82.   **Retrun To Suining**

To the Tune of Xi Chun Lai
(Glad to Welcome the Spring)
Suining, Sichuan
July 27, 1981

My dream of thirty years to depart
Is over,
Like a flowing river.
I, a victorious soldier, fifty years of age,
Now come home.
I am entirely unaware
Of the war situation of the native land.
I implore the Holy Son:
Let me fly to the West soon!

83. 痛悉聶冀道神父
出獄後病逝

漁歌子
遂寧
1981 年 8 月 17 日

「三自」聲稱倡最先，

依然下獄十餘年。

為獄友，

暑寒三。

永安慨賜望蒼天！

83.   Sadly Learning
The Death Of Illness of Fr. Nie Jidao
After His Release From Prison

To the Tune of Yu Ge Zi
(The Fisherman's Song)
Suining
August 17, 1981

You had professed, Fr. Nie,
That you were the first one
Who had initiated the "Three-Selfs."
Yet,
You were still thrown into prison
For over ten years.
We were fellow inmates
In the same prison
For three summers and winters.
I hope
That Heave will generously
Grant you eternal rest!

84. 往訪
愛國教會本堂黃渥澤神父
查閱彌撒經書
藉以弄清
一些慶節的確切日期

調笑令
遂寧
1981 年 9 月 27 日

堂殿，

堂殿，

查閱經書拜見。

主人未晤多年，

顏新**赤縣**變天，

天變，

天變，

難遇忠貞腸斷！

84.   Visiting The Patriotic Pastor, Fr. Huang Woze, To Consult The Missal To Find Out The Exact Dates Of Some Liturgical Feasts

To the Tune of Tiao Xiao Ling
(Making a Joke)
Suining
September 27, 1981

To the chapel,
To the chapel
I pay a visit
On purpose to consult the missal.
I have missed my host
For many years;
His face has become new,
Since the change of the sky of China.
The sky has changed,
Ths sky has changed;
Rarely meeting a loyal Catholic,
I am broken-hearted!

85. 旋里兩月

漁家傲
遂寧
1981 年 9 月 27 日

三十年來同**敵**戰，
神兵奏凱家園返。
本想從今離火線，
居後院，
高飛遠走深盤算。

家外家中憂患滿，
朝朝暮暮來磨練。
振作精神迎萬變。
天意善，
苦杯斟飲無尤怨！

85.   Two Months
After Returning Home

To the Tune of Yu Jia Ao
(Fisherman's Pride)
Suining
September 27, 1981

Having battled with the enemy for thirty years,
I, the Divine Warrior,
Triumphantly returned to my family.
I thought:
I would leave the front line from then on,
I would live in the backyard,
Figuring carefully
How to fly far and high to a distant region.

In the house and outside
Many troubles and hardships
Have tempered me day and night.
I strive to bestir myself
To meet all the changes.
The Will of Heaven is good;
I will drink the cup of bitterness
Without blame and complaint!

86. 水災

五言詩
遂寧
1981 年 9 月 29 日

滂沱持續降，
洪水流湯湯。
城鄉成澤國，
數省遭禍殃。

好多房田毀？
幾許死和傷？
庶民長受苦，
赤政暴如常。

假我以神勇，
當面譴**赤狼**：
「時日害喪乎？
予及女偕亡！」

86.   Floods

In the Poetic Style of Wuyan Shi
Suining
September 29, 1981

Under a continuous and torrential rainfall,
The floods have flowed.
Many towns and countrysides have become submerged,
Several provinces have suffered disasters.

How many houses and fields have been destroyed?
How many casualities are there?
Common people are subjected to privations
For such a long time;
Yet,
The Red dictatorship remains tyrannical as usual.

If I had extraordinary bravery,
I would go to rebuke the Red wolf face to face:
"Why should not you, this sun, perish?
I would like to die together with you!"

87. 題照
賀二姪女周仲玉主保節

五言詩

遂寧

1981 年 10 月 1 日

聖女嬰孩耶穌德蘭節

忽忽三十年，
呱呱墜地生。
秉承先祖命，
付洗復起名。

別猶搖籃臥，
歸已娘親成。
曲折人生路，
興奮重逢情。

遵循祖父訓，
牢記上主恩。
殊途而同歸，
祝願獻良辰！

87.   Dedication On A Photo To Congratulate Theresa Zhou Zhongyu, My Second Niece, On Her Feastday

In The Poetic Style of Wuyan Shi
Suining
October 1, 1981
Feast of St. Theresa of the Child Jesus

How fast
Thirty years have passed
Since you came into the world with a cry!
By the order of your late grandfather,
I baptized you
And gave you this holy name.

At my departure,
You still lay in a cradle;
On my return,
You have already become a mother.
The road of life is tortuous,
The feelings of reunion is ardent.

You must follow
The instructions of your grandfather,
You must keep well
The graces of the Lord in your heart.
We will reach the same goal
By different routes:
This is my best wish to you
On this your brilliant Feastday!

88. 祝鐵窗好友傳志雄
前程錦繡

四言詩
遂寧
1981 年 10 月 4 日

四年同獄，
初若路人。
年青有為，
來學英文

八月切磋，
情厚誼殷。
未幾獲釋，
抱負欲伸。

我亦旋踵，
跨出監門。
魚雁屢通，
近況喜聞。

剛剛不久，
邀訪諄諄；
回函告以，
難於抽身。

來朝晤否？
重重疑雲。
前程錦繡，
良願獻君！

88.   A Glorious Future To Mr. Fu Zhixiong, My Good Friend In Prison

In the Poetic Style of Siyan Shi
Suining
October 4, 1981

We were in the same jail for four years.
During the first period,
We treated each other like a passerby.
You, a young and promising man,
Came to me to learn English.

We studied together for eight months,
Forming a deep friendship.
Before long you were released,
Hoping to spread your high aspirations.

Shortly I also walked out the prison gates.
I wrote you several times;
I was glad to know your current situation.

Just recently,
I invited sincerely your visit;
You gave an answer saying that
It would be hard for you to get away.

Whether we will meet again or not in the future,
It is totally uncertain.
A glorious future —
This is my best wish to you!

89. 夢碎

憶江南
遂寧
1981 年 10 月 7 日

收匯票，
昨夜夢魂欣。
和日今猶升又落，
未嘗見到報音人！
夢碎豈眉顰？

89.   A Dream Shattered

To the Tune of Yi Jiang Nan
(Temembering the South of the River)
Suining
October 7, 1981

Upon receiving a bank draft,
My heart was cheerful
In the dream last night.
Today,
The mild sun
Still rises up and sets down;
Yet,
I have not seen the messenger come!
For the dream shattered,
Should I knit my brows?

90. 人大常委會委員長 葉劍英先生關於 台灣問題的講話讀後

更漏子
遂寧
1981 年 10 月 10 日

玉山登，
雲海望，
中共卅年常想。
威儘用，
效難生，
向隅空涕零！

條款九，
陰謀售，
寶島欲吞依舊。
譏善義，
駁賢儒，
有誰會謟諛？

90.   After Reading The Talk On The Issue Of Taiwan By Mr. Ye jianying, The President Of The Standing Committee Of The National People's Congress

To the Tune of Geng Lou Zi
(The Hourglass)
Suining
October 10, 1981

To climb the Mount Yushan,
To Look over the sea of clouds,
This the Chinese Communists have yearned for
Over thirty years.
Having resorted to threats,
They did not achieve any result;
They vainly cry all alone in a corner!

Now,
Offering the Nine Articles,
They try to peddle their plots,
Hoping as before to gobble the Precious Island.
The good and the righteous will mock,
The sage and the learned will rebuke.
Who will fawn on them?

91.　諸聖節

憶秦娥
遂寧
1981 年 11 月 1 日

晨風冽，
河堤漫步迎佳節。
迎佳節，
唸經崇主，
頌歌賢哲。

長遭佔據堂嗚咽，
發還今日人心悅。
人心悅，
吃羊狼性，
豈真湮滅？

91   All Saints Day

To the Tune of Yi Qin E
(Remembering the Beauty of Qin)
Suining
November 1, 1981

In the cool morning breeze,
I stroll on the river's embankment
To welcome the happy Feast.
To welcome the happy Feast,
I say my prayers to worship the Lord
And to sing the praises
Of the saints, virtuous and wise.

Long occupied,
The sacred chapel sobbed.
Today,
It is given back.
The feelings of the people are glad.
The feelings of the prople are glad,
Yet,
The Wolf's nature of eating sheep,
Can such a trait disappear?

92. 《人民日報》
譴責美國喬治亞州州長
贊助台灣

桂殿秋
遂寧
1981 年 11 月 17 日

洶惡浪，
砥中流！
豪情州長照千秋！
北京舌劍徒揮舞，
赤縣終將獲自由！

92.   The *People's Daily* Reproaches The Governor Of Georgia In The USA For His Support of Taiwan

To the Tune of Gui Dian Qiu
(Autumn in the Cassia Hall)
Suining
November 17, 1981

In the surging wicked waves,
Behold,
A firm rock standing in midstream!
My dear Governor,
Your lofty sentiments shine for ages!
Beijing brandishes its verbal swords
To no avail,
China will ultimately gain freedom!

93. 回家四月

摸魚兒
遂寧
1981 年 11 月 27 日

百餘天，
家園歸返，
片時歡樂雲散。
筆耕攻讀常遭阻，
生活苦酸充滿。
尤可歎，
為陷害、
兄來暗竊私書翰。
逼欺辱譴，
好似影隨形，
家常便飯。
熱淚浥雙眼！

緣何在？
拒事牛頭馬面，
堅從真理至善。

93.   Four Months After Homecoming

To the Tune of Mo Yu'er
(Trying to Catch Fish)
Suining
November 27, 1981

Over one hundred days
Since my homecoming,
My joy of a short while has vanished
As melting clouds.
My writing and reading are always hindered;
My life is filled with bitterness.
A particular sigh of regret:
To frame me up,
My brother secretly stole my private letters.
His pressing, bullying, insulting and blaming
Accompany me
Like the shadow following the person,
Like all in a day's work.
My eyes were wet with bitter tears!

What was the reason for this?
I refused to serve the monsters,
But I firmly followed
The Truth and the Supreme Good.

操戈同室因**基督**，
主訓真知高見。
懷善願，
扶弱小、
嫂來緩解來相勸。
皇天禱獻：
海外信相通，
來秋風起，
逃出好孤雁！

We, two brothers, quarrel with each other,
For the sake of Christ;
Thus,
The instructions of the Lord give
Real knowledge and deep insight.
Harboring good intentions,
Supporting the weak,
My sister-in-law came
To soften and to advise.
I offer my prayers to High Heaven:
With correspondence from abroad,
In the coming fall,
When the west wind rises,
As a solitary goose,
I may fly away!

94. 柬埔寨共產黨
被迫宣佈解散

搗練子
遂寧
1981 年 12 月 10 日

行恐怖，
害人民，
無數冤魂冥府呻。
罪惡滔天招眾怒，
自行掘墓葬尊身！

94.   The Cambodian Communist Party Is Compelled To Declare Its Dissolution

To the Tune of Dao Lian Zi
(Pounding Silk Floss)
Suining
December 10, 1981

Having carried out terror,
You, Cambodian Communists,
Have done your people great harm.
Countless souls of the injured victims sob
In the nether regions.
Your monstrous crimes provoked public wrath.
Now,
You have to bury your hideous bodies
In the graves dug with your own hands!

95.　赴蓉訪友

七律
成都
1981 年 12 月 22 日

啟程清早霧茫茫，
午後晴空抵錦江。
離別念年心鬱鬱，
重遊今日意揚揚。
無榮灑下賤軀血，
有幸重登故友堂。
往事舊情難敘述，
待償願望攪愁腸！

95.   Going To Chengdu
To Visit My Friends

In the Poetic Style of Qilu
Chengdu
December 22, 1981

In the early morning,
I set out on my journey
In a dense fog.
In the afternoon,
I arrived to the Jin Jiang, to Chengdu,
Under clear sky.
I was melancholy
For our twenty-year separation;
Now I rejoice in my return.
Not granted the glory
Of shedding my blood,
I have the good fortune
Of calling the house of my old friends.
It is hard
To narrate the past events and old feelings;
Waiting to be fulfilled,
My wishes disturb my worried heart!

96. 訪老戰友
舒德君修女

五律
成都
1981 年 12 月 28 日

久別重逢日，
錦江冬已深。
立功狼抗昔，
變色虎談今。
雨雪貞花毀，
風霜壯志侵！
耳聞惟數語，
難悉爾芳心！

96.   A Visit To
An Old Battle Companion,
Sr. Lucia Shu Dejun

In the Poetic Style of Wulu
Chengdu
December 28, 1981

After a long separation,
This day,
In the depth of winter,
We meet again
In the Jin Jiang, in Chengdu.
During former times
You made contributions
In combating the Wolf;
Today,
You turn pale
At the mention of the Tiger.
Rain and snow have destroyed
The flower of your chastity;
Wind and frost have corroded
Your lofty ideals!
Hearing from you only a few words,
I am unable to know
More about your innermost fragrant heart!

97. 晤老戰友
雷靜淵修女

七絕
成都
1981 年 12 月 29 日

相處兩冬受益深，
赤妖勇抗顯雄心。
多年**教難**煎熬受，
知己適人淚滿襟！

97.   Meeting With Sr. Anna Lei Jingyuan, An Old Comrade-In-Arms

In the Poetic Style of Qijue
Chengdu
December 29, 1981

Getting along with each other
Through two winters,
I benefited from you very much.
You showed a lofty aspiration
In resisting bravely the Red devil.
During the long years
Of the religious persecution,
You suffered much torment.
Learning that you had gotten married,
My tears bedew my coat!

98. 辭別舊歲

浣溪沙
成都
1981 年 12 月 31 日

拒購毛書判五秋。
三回申訴錯終糾,
出牢返里喜心頭。

釜豆箕煎誰料及?
愁懷舒展錦城遊。
精神重振戰貔貅!

98.   Bidding Farewell
To The Outgoing Year

To the Tune of Huan Xi Sha
(Yarn Washed in the Stream)
Chengdu
December 31, 1981

Because of my refusal to buy Mao's book,
I was sentenced to five more autumns.
Through my three appeals
I got my misjudged case
Redressed at long last.
I rejoiced
At leaving the jail and coming home.

Who would have imagined
That the beanstalk would cook the bean?
To relax my anxious mind,
I came on trips to Chengdu.
I must once more exert myself
To struggle with the fierce Beast!

99. 喜晤老戰友
陳敏德修女

七絕
成都
1982 年 1 月 3 日

昔戰狂瀾多激昂！
瀾仍洶湧意惶惶。
從前送別情深厚，
今又窖中示慨慷。

99.　Joyful To See
Sr. Chen Minde,
An Old Battle Companion

In the Poetic Style of Qijue
Chengdu
January 3, 1982

In past days,
When you battled with the raging waves,
How impassioned you were!
Now, the waves are still tempestuous,
You are anxious.
Once, you came to see me off,
Expressing your deep affection.
This time,
You show me your generosity
In my sorry plight.

100. 告別
蕭濟醫生
和郎毓秀教授

四言詩
成都
1982 年 1 月 5 日

捍衛**聖教**，
自由樂捐；
與世隔絕，
二十六年。

靠**主**助祐，
終奏凱旋。
還鄉境窘，
鬥志仍堅。

樂壇盛名，
累載報刊。
冒昧修書，
祈解倒懸。

100.   Taking Leave Of Doctor Michel Xiao Ji And Professor Pansy Lang Yuxiu

In the Poetic Style of Siyan Shi
Chengdu
January 5, 1982

To defend our Holy Church,
I have gladly relinquished my liberty.
I had been cut off
From the outside world
For twenty-six years.

With the help of the Lord,
I won the victory at last.
When I returned to my native place
I was in a very sorry plight,
But my fighting will is still firm.

Since you, Pansy, enjoy a great reputation
In the music world,
Your name frequently appears in the press.
I took the liberty to write you,
Asking help
To relieve me from my sore straits.

秋送冬迎，
終讀華箋；
承蒙邀訪，
聖誕節前。

尊府榮登，
樂也陶然。
音容長輩，
一若當年。

風霜飽飲，
仍執教鞭。
兒孫滿堂，
天倫敘歡。

院友天涯，
音訊為傳。
專刊讓看，
睹其今顏。

與之相隔，
萬水千山。

Having seen the fall off
And welcoming the winter in,
I ultimately read your esteemed letter.
I was granted an invitation to visit
Before the Solemnity of Christmas.

Having the honor of coming to your house,
I felt contented and happy.
The voices and countenances of both of you,
My venerable elders,
Are just as in those past days.

In spite of being weather-beaten,
You, Pansy, are still engaged in teaching.
Your family is full of children and grandchildren;
You have the joys
Of a family living and conversing together.

My fellow monastic brothers are
As far away as the end of the earth;
You bring me their messages.
You let me read the special anniversary issue
And see their present faces.

I am separated from them
By ten thousand rivers and a thousand mountains.

豈易前往？
豈易團圓？

長夜漫漫，
錦水湍湍，
故舊散亡，
少晤心酸。

半月府上，
關照周全；
蒙賜訓誨，
蒙解疑難。

煩擾令受，
深感汗顏。
告辭在即，
謝意拳拳。

求主以愛，
常潤心田；
猶祈保重，
再見來天！

Is it possible to go there?
Is it easy to rejoin them?

After a very long night,
With the Jin Jiang surging on,
Old friends and acquaintances here
Are scattered or dead.
I am grieved
To have met so few of them.

During my half-a-month stay
In your house,
You have shown me a deep loving care.
You have also given me some instructions
And removed some of my doubts and difficulties.

Thinking that I have bothered and disturbed you,
I blush with shame.
Nearing my departure,
I offer you my sincere gratitude.

I entreat the Lord
To always moisten your hearts with His love.
I also earnestly hope
That you take good care of yourselves.
Finally,
I wish to see you again some day!

One day in the autumn of 1948, Professor Sun Fuyuan, the secretary of Fr. Prior Raphael Vinciarelli and our teacher of Chinese literature, seated with his girl student by the gate of the small parlor of the Chengdu Monastery.

1948年秋季的一天，既是文嘉禮院長的秘書，也是我們的中國文學老師的孫伏園教授，同他的一位女學生，坐在成都修院小客廳門邊。

A picture in his baptism, a souvenir of Ye Jun, a student of Fr. Eleutherius Winance in the Sichuan Provincial Academy of Arts, taken in the courtyard of the Chengdu Monastery on September 8, 1948. (L-R): (front row) classmate, Vincent Yuan Nengding, classmate, Andrew Ye Jun, Dcotor Michel Xiao Ji, his godfather, 2 classmates; (back row) Fr. Eleutherius, Luke Li Youxing, his President, Fr. Emile, a local diocesan French priest, Fr. Alberic and Fr. Prior Raphael.

1948年9月8日，華倫士神父在四川省立藝術專科學校的學生葉俊，領洗後攝於成都修院庭園的紀念照。（左起）：（前排）他的同學、袁能鼎、同學、葉俊、代父蕭濟醫生、同學、同學；（後排）華神父、李有行校長、本地教區法國神父、孔神父和文院長。

One day in the early summer of 1949, Fr. Thaddeus Yang Anran (R) with Doctor Michel Xiao Ji in the courtyard of the Chengdu Monastery.

1949 年初夏的一天，楊安然神父（右）和蕭濟醫生在成都修院的庭園內。

In early December 1949, Doctor Michel Xiao Ji and his wife, soprano Pansy Lang Yuxiu with their 4 children visit the Chengdu Monastery, taken in front of the new building. (L-R): Vincent Yuan Nengding, Fr. Alberic, Fr. Prior Raphael, Fr. Emile, Pansy Lang, Michel Xiao, Fr. Hildebrand, Fr. Werner and the 4 children.

1949年12月初，蕭濟醫生和其妻女高音歌唱家郎毓秀，帶著四個孩子來成都修院探望。合影於新樓房前面。（左起）：袁能鼎、孔神父、文院長、武神父、郎女士、蕭醫生、馬神父、白神父和四個小孩。

In the late 1950s, Fr. Prior Paphael Vinciarelli (C), Fr. Vincent de Martin (L) and Fr. Felix Tang Tianshou (R) seated in the meadow in St. Andrew's Priory, Valyermo, CA, USA.

20世紀50年代晚期，文嘉禮院長（中）、丁谷鳴神父（左）和唐天壽神父（右），坐在美國加州化野漢聖安德肋修院的草地上。

On November 12, 1981, Zhou Zhonglan, the second niece of Br. Peter in Taiwan, is answering the phone in their home, on her wedding day.

1981年11月12日，筆者在台灣的二姪女周仲蘭在家中接電話。那天正是她的婚禮日。

*Br. Peter in Suining County
in Sichuan Province, China,
on December 28, 1982.*

1982年12月28日，筆者在
中國四川省遂寧縣。

*A picture taken on October 6, 1984, as a parting
souvenir, from John Baptist Huang Xinzhu (Zifu)
and Theresa Xiao Likun, a married couple, Br.
Peter's close friends in Suining.*

筆者在遂寧的好友，黃辛竹（自扶）和蕭莉琨
伉儷拍於1984年10月6日的臨別紀念照。

*On October 14, 1984, Br. Peter strolls
the Gugong (the Imperial Palace)
Museum in Beijing.*

1984年10月14日，筆者遊覽了北京
故宮博物院。

256

On October 23, 1984, Br. Peter tours the Yiheyuan (the Summer Palace) in Beijing.

1984 年10月23日，筆者遊了北京頤和園（夏宮）。

On May 14, 1985, Br. Peter (L) with Fr. Jerome Neufelder, a German guest for half a year, by the monastic chapel.

1985 年5月14日，筆者(左)與作客半年的熱羅尼莫‧內費爾德德國神父，合影於修院聖堂傍。

Br. Peter standing beside the Statue of Our Lady Of Fatima, taken by Fr. Subprior Neal G. Roth on October 13, 1985, when Br. Peter visited for the first time St. Martin's Abbey in Lacey, Oregon.

筆者站在法蒂瑪聖母雕像傍，由尼爾‧羅特副院長拍攝於1985年10月13日，當筆者初次拜訪俄勒岡州萊西聖瑪爾定大修院時。

November 27, 1985, on Thanksgiving Day, Br. Peter (first left), Diane Ferris (second left), an English teacher, and classmates at the dinner party in the classroom in Clackamas Community College in Oregon City, Oregon. (taken by Ann, a classmate).

1985年11月27日感恩節，筆者（左一）、英語教師黛安・費里斯（左二）和同班同學們在俄勒岡州俄勒岡市克拉克瑪社區學院的教室裡聚餐（由同學安拍攝）。

A wedding picture in December 1985 of Ms. Molly Williams, then one of Br. Peter's English teachers in Clackamas Community College in Oregon City, Oregon.

莫利・威廉斯女士1985年12月的結婚照，她是筆者當時在俄勒岡州俄勒岡市克拉克瑪社區學院的一位英語教師。

On October 29, 1986, at 1:00 pm, Br. Peter is embraced and kissed in St. Peter's Square in Rome by Pope John Paul II in greeting the people at the close of his Wednesday general audience.

1986年10月29日，午後一點，筆者於羅馬聖伯多祿廣場，蒙受教宗若望保祿二世在星期三接見公眾將終的巡視時的擁抱和親吻。

On October 30, 1986, at 7:30 am, Br. Peter (in the left corner) attends the Mass Holy Father John Paul II celebrates in his private chapel in the apostolic palace in the Vatican.

1986年10月30日清早7點半,筆者在梵蒂岡宗座宮廷私人小堂的左邊角落處,望了聖父若望保祿二世舉行的彌撒。

On October 30, 1986, at 8:30 am, having heard the Mass of Pope John Paul II, Br. Peter kneels before him in receiving the gift, a rosary, in the audience room in the apostobic palace, Vatican.

1986年10月30日清早8點半,筆者在聽完教宗若望保祿二世的彌撒後,於梵蒂岡宗座宮廷觀見室,跪在他面前領取禮品——念珠。

On November 26, 1986, in the evening, Br. Peter (second left), while residing temporarily in Brussels, Belgium, is invited to their family dinner by Miss Marie Alghisi (first left) and her parents, Primo and Genevieve.

1986年11月26日晚上,筆者(左二)在比利時布魯塞爾客居期間,應瑪利亞‧阿爾吉西小姐(左一)和她雙親普里莫與熱納維埃夫的邀請,往赴家宴。

A photograph of Diane Richardson at Christmas, December 25, 1986, with her husband, Douglas, and their son, Bob. She lives in Milwaukie, Oregon, and is Br. Peter's good friend and constant correspondent since December 1985.

黛安・理查森和其夫君道格拉斯與兒子鮑勃1986年12月25日的聖誕節照。她住在俄勒岡州密爾沃基，是筆者自1985年12月以來的好友和經常的通信者。

Br. Peter with his good friends, Leo and Amy Greenwood from Sepulveda, CA; taken in the monastery lounge on May 31, 1988.

筆者和來自加州塞普爾維達市的好友良與艾米・格林伍德，在1988年5月31日，合影於修院客廳。

On June 18, 1988, Br. Peter meets in the monastery lounge his visitors: Fr. Jerome J. Heyndrickx, CICM (C), from Belgium, and Mr. Mickael L. Cotter (R).

1988年6月18日，筆者在修院客廳會見了來訪客人：比利時籍韓德力神父（中）和彌額爾・科特先生（右）。

On June 18, 1988, Br. Peter (C) with his visitors, Fr. Jerome (R) and Miss Elaine Huang Huiling (L) from Taiwan, the fiancee of Michael Cotter, on the monastery grounds.

1988 年6月18日，筆者（中）和訪客韓德力神父（右）與彌額爾‧科特的來自台灣的未婚妻黃慧玲小姐（左）合影於修院場地。

On June 25, 1988, Br. Peter (C) with his good Indonesian friends, Philippus H. and Flora Luciana Herkata, a married couple; taken on the monastery grounds.

1988 年6月25日，筆者（中）和印度尼西亞好友斐理伯與弗洛拉‧露西婭娜‧赫凱塔伉儷，合影於修院場地。

On March 5, 1989, Br. Peter (R) with his good friends: Jean DeBettignies (L), his sponsor, and Terry Thompson (C), his volunteer typist, taken on the monastery grounds.

1989年3月5日，筆者（右）與其好友：吉恩‧德‧貝蒂尼（左）贊助者和特麗‧湯普森（中）打字義工，合影於修院場地。

On April 30, 1989, Br. Peter with his good Korean friend, Miss Marianna So, on the monastery grounds.

1989年4月30日，筆者和韓國好友徐美仙小姐合影於修院場地。

Mr. Sam Raber, Br. Peter's good Jewish friend, in the monastery cemetery, November 7, 1989.

筆者猶太好友薩姆‧雷伯老先生，1989年11月7日攝影於修院墓地。

Br. Peter's good friend, Jeff Kouf, his wife, Mary, and son, William, taken in December 1989. In early 1990, Jeff made his effort to help me seeking a publisher for my first book.

筆者好友杰弗‧科福和他的太太瑪利亞、兒子威廉，1989年12月的全家福。杰弗曾在1990年初努力幫助我，爲我的頭本書尋找出版者。

On March 24, 1991, Br. Peter with his good friends, Jim and Jeannine Veraldi, a married couple, in the monastery lounge.

筆者和好友吉姆與詹寧‧維拉爾迪伉儷，1991年3月24日合影於修院客廳。

On April 8, 1992, at the request of Br. Peter, his old classmate in Taiwan, James Mao Yongchang, visits his good friend, Sr. Grace Ye Suzhen, SDSH, in the convent in Taipei City.

1992年4月8日，筆者在台灣的老同學毛永昌，應請去看望了他在台北市耶穌聖心修女院的好友葉素貞修女。

On June 1, 1992, Br. Peter meets in the monastery with a visitor, Br. Lucas He Jintang, born in Hong Kong, a brother in the Taize Community in France.

1992年6月1日，筆者在修院會見了生於香港的訪客何錦棠弟兄，他是法國泰澤團體的一位成員。

On June 2, 1992, Fr. Eleutherius Winance (C) joins Br. Peter's (R) meeting with Br. Lucas He Jintang (L).

1992 年6月2日，華倫士神父（中）參加了筆者（右）與何錦棠弟兄（左）的會見。

On September 27, 1992, during the monastery's 36th Valyermo Fall Festival, Br. Peter (C) with his publisher, Jim Moeller (R), and his editor, Cynthia Clark (L), in front of his book booth, selling his just-published books.

1992 年9月27日，在修院的36 屆化野漢秋節期間，筆者（中）和他的出版者吉姆·莫勒（右）與審訂者辛西婭·克拉克（左），合影於售賣他剛出版的書的攤位前。

On July 16, 1993, when Br. Peter stays in their house as a guest for a week, his hosts, Hugo and Irene Foertsch, a married couple, take him to tour Disneyland on the outskirts of Los Angeles.

1993年7月16日，當筆者在雨果和艾琳·福爾斯伉儷家作客一週時，主人帶筆者去遊覽了洛杉磯郊外的迪斯尼遊樂園。

On July 16, 1993, Br. Peter with his hostess Irene in Disneyland; Br. Peter (R) with his host Hugo (L) in Disneyland (in the picture above).

1993 年7月16日，筆者和女主人艾琳在迪斯尼遊樂園中；上圖那張照片，是筆者（右）與男主人雨果（左）在遊樂園的合影。

On August 8, 1993, James Mao Yongchang, Br. Peter's old classmate, visits the chapel of their former Xishan monastery in Nanchong in Sichuan Proxvince.

1993年8月8日，筆者的老同學毛永昌參觀了他們從前在四川省南充的西山修院的聖堂。

On February 6, 1994, Fr. Werner Papeians (L) and Br. Peter (R) meet in the monastery with Richard J. Chacon (C), Professor of Anthropology in El Camino College in Torrance in California.

1994 年2月6日，白微明神父（左）和筆者（右）在修院會見了加利學福尼亞州托倫斯市埃爾‧卡米諾學院人類學教授理查德‧蔡康（中）。

On April 9, 1994, Br. Peter (L) and
Fr. Werner Papeians (R) with their
old friend far from China, Dr.
Michel Xiao Ji (second left), in the
monastery cemetery.

1994 年4月9日，筆者（左）與
白徵明神父（右），和他們來自
中國的好友蕭濟醫生（左二），
合影於修院墓地。

A 1995 photograph of the whole family of
Br. Peter's good Korean friends, Paul and
Christina Kim with their two daughters;
(L-R) Amanda, Christina, Paul and Jennifer.

筆者的韓國好友金明天和金純熙，與他們
兩個女兒1995年的全家福；（左起）阿曼
達、金純熙、金明天和詹妮弗。

On July 16, 1995, Br. Peter (L)
with Dana Peters (R), a press
photographer, on the monastery
grounds.

筆者和攝影記者達納‧彼得斯，
1995 年7月16日合影於修院場
地。

On May 22, 1997, James Mao Yongchang (R),
Br. Peter's old classmate in Taiwan, goes to
Taipei City to meet with Fr. Vincent Martin (L)
staying as a guest in a Benedictine monastery.

1997年5月22日，筆者在台灣的老同學毛永
昌（右）去台北市拜會了客居於一座本篤
會修院的丁谷鳴神父（左）。

On May 28, 1997, James Mao Yongchang (L)
in Taiwan, Br. Peter's old classmate, takes Fr.
Vincent Martin (C) to go to Longtan Township
in Taoyuan County to call on Br. Peter's fifth-
elder brother, Philip Zhou Zhimin (R).

1997 年5月28日，筆者在台灣的老同學
毛永昌（左），帶領丁谷鳴神父（中），
往桃園縣龍潭鄉，探望了筆者的五哥
周止民（右）。

On December 3, 1997, Br. Peter with his
good friend, Madonna Edgar and her
youngest son Jake, taken in front of the
Abbey Bookshop.

1997年12月3日，筆者與好友瑪丹娜‧
埃德加和她最小的孩子杰克，拍於修
院書店門前。

On December 25, 1997, Br. Peter joins once
again the family Christmas gathering of his
good Philippine friends in Burbank, CA;
(R-L) Jaime Abrera, Br. Peter, Joseph, Janine,
Jainee (died on July 16, 2004), Audrey Abrera
and her mother, Lora Verenice (died on March
26, 2005).

1997年12月25日，筆者又一次參加了加州
柏班克市菲律賓好友的聖誕家庭聚會。
（右起）杰姆‧阿伯雷拉、筆者、若瑟、
杰寧、杰妮（2004年7月16日去世）、奧
德麗‧阿伯雷拉和她的母親洛拉‧維雷尼
斯（2005年3月26日去世）。

On October 15, 2000, during the dinner in
celebration on the Golden Jubilee of his
monastic profession, Br. Peter with his good
friends, Mr. Frederick (died on December 1,
2008) and Mrs. Barbara Clement.

2000年10月15日，筆者在其矢發修會誓願
五十週年金慶的宴會中，與好友弗雷德里
克‧克萊門特先生（2008年12月1日去世）
和巴巴拉太太合影。

On May 2, 2001, at 7:30am, Br. Peter (in the
right corner) attends the Mass of Pope John
Paul II in his private chapel in the apostolic
palace in the Vatican.

2001年5月2日清早七點半鐘，筆者（右邊
角落）在梵蒂岡宗座宮廷的私人小堂，望
了教宗若望保祿二世的彌撒。

On May 2, 2001, in the morning after Mass, Br. Peter presents to the Pope his three books in the audience hall.

2001年5月2日清早彌撒後，筆者在接見廳向教宗呈獻了他的三本書。

On May 2, 2001, in the afternoon, Br. Peter and Audrey Abrera, his good Philippine friend and traveling companion, visit St. Paul Basilica in Rome.

2001年5月2日，筆者和他的菲律賓好友與旅伴奧德麗‧阿伯雷拉，參觀了羅馬聖祿大殿。

On May 2, 2001, in the afternoon, Br. Peter (L) and Jaime Abrera (R), his good Philippine friend and traveling companion, visit St. Paul Basilica in Rome.

2001年5月2日，筆者和他的菲律賓好友與旅伴杰姆‧阿伯雷拉，參觀了羅馬聖祿大殿。

101. 還鄉半年

七律
遂寧
1982 年 1 月 17 日

覆信前秋兄語摯，
歸來去夏亦欣迎。
「革新」見拒龍顏怒，
就業關懷外表誠。
讀寫起居吾忐忑，
欺凌斥辱彼猙獰。
境艱豈可初衷改，
勇搏方能風浪平！

101.   Returning To My Home Town For Half A Year

In the Poetic Style of Qilu
Suining
January 27, 1982

In his answer
To my letter of the fall before last,
My brother's words were sincere.
Last summer when I came back,
He gave me also a joyful welcome.
Seeing my refusal
To the religious Reform,
He showed me an angry look,
Like an imperial dragon's face.
About my employment
He paid only an apparent concern.
I was fidgety
In reading, writing and daily living;
He has displayed ferocious features
In bullying, blaming and insulting me.
In this difficult situation,
How could I change my original intentions?
Through boldly wrestling,
The wind and waves
Can subside and be calmed!

102. 衛青心神父來信
讀後一月

七律
遂寧
1982 年 2 月 6 日

月前返里尊函閱，
窘迫心情實激昂。
惠譯拙箋欣院長，
慨施教導勵忠腸。
回書兩度言由義，
候駕四週愁滿腔。
信鴿豈遭鷹獵取？
或緣異夢與同床？

102. One Month After Reading The Letter Of Fr. Louis Wei Qingxin

In the Poetic Style of Qilu
Suining
February 6, 1982

Upon my return last month,
I read your venerable letter,
Feeling really excited
In my embarrassed heart.
Your gracious interpretation of my letter
Gladdened Fr. Abbot Michael Coune.
Your kind instructions encouraged me,
A Catholic with a loyal heart.
I wrote you back twice
With serious words,
With the force of justice.
My heart has been filled
With worries for four weeks
In awaiting your promised visit.
Has the homing pigeon been hunted
By the eagle?
Or,
Do we dream different dreams,
Though sharing the same bed of Faith?

103. 偶遇昔日獄友
辛大榮

搗練子
南充
1982 年 2 月 12 日

三載獄，
共霜風，
邂逅果州欲盡冬。
呼喊熱情還邀訪，
重溫舊誼樂融融。

103.   Coming Across Mr. Xin Darong, A Former Fellow Prisoner

To the Tune of Dao Lian Zi
(Pounding Silk Floss)
Nanchong
February 12, 1982

For three years in jail
We tasted together the frost and the wind.
At the time
When the winter is near to closing,
I run into you by chance
In Nancong.
You call me warmly by name,
You even invite me
To pay you a visit.
I much exult
In reliving our old friendship.

104. 前往果監蓬營
申請返歸就業

七律
遂寧
1982 年 2 月 16 日

兄家難以此身棲，
風雨乘車果郡馳。
錦鎮蓬營當面拒，
河東果獄補償貽。
枯殘右手百圓領，
冷酷家園六日歸。
就業住房依舊渺，
如何為主戰熊羆？

104.   Going To The Nanchong Prison And The Peng'an Camp To Apply For Return And Employment

In the Poetic Style of Qilu
Suining
February 16, 1982

It is difficult
To stay in my brother's house.
In wind and in rain
I rode in a bus to Nanchong.
The Peng'an camp in Jinping
Refused my application to my face,
While the Nanchong jail in Hedong
Gave me a compensation.
For my withered right hand
I got one hundred dollars.
Six days later,
I returned to my unfeeling family.
My employment and housing
Are still uncertain.
How should I fight the Bear
For the Lord?

105. 題書《新華字典》
贈唐天壽神父

七絕
遂寧
1982 年 2 月 28 日

別恨離愁近卅年，
今知健壯樂陶然。
猶新記憶往時景，
舊事重提月早圓！

105.   Dedication On The Book, *Xin Hua Dictionary*, To Fr. Felix Tang Tianshou

In the Poetic Style of Qijue
Suining
February 28, 1982

Our parting grief and sorrow
Have lasted almost forty years.
I am overjoyed
In knowing
That you are still healthy and strong.
The scenes of the old times
Remain fresh in my memory.
To recall our past events,
I hope
The moon will be full soon!

106. 再訪
郎毓秀教授

浣溪沙
成都
1982 年 3 月 4 日

工作尋求近況陳，
良謀善策欲親聞，
征程再啟錦江奔。

濃霧晨空終散盡，
春陽高照暖心身，
殷殷期望沐天恩。

106.   My Second Visit To Professor Pansy Lang Yuxiu

To the Tune of Huan Xi Sha
(Yarn Washed in the Stream)
Chengdu
March 4, 1982

To seek a job,
To report on my recent development,
And to hear personally
Her good guidance and wise proposal,
I set out on a journey
To Chengdu once again.

Dense fogs in the morning sky
Finally disappear totally.
The spring sun shines over me,
Warming my heart and my body.
I hope eagerly
To be steeped in the divine favor.

107. 訪昔日戰友
賈志中先生

清平樂
成都
1982 年 3 月 5 日

無家影隻，
身困心憂悒。
兄長還鄉神志失，
聞告衣衫淚濕！

當年志氣消亡，
身心今日淒涼。
持續卅冬風暴，
仍堅怎易忠良?!

107.   Visiting Mr. Jia Zhizhong, A Former Battle Companion

To the Tune of Qing Ping Yue
(The Qing Ping Song)
Chengdu
March 5, 1982

He is homeless,
Extremely lonely as a single shadow.
His body is tired,
His heart is anxious.
Having been back to his native place,
His brother has lost his right mind.
Hearing of this,
Tears bedew my coat!

His aspiration in those years
Has run away.
Today,
He is dreary in body and mind.
The storm has lasted thirty winters;
How is it easy
For a loyal catholic
To remain stll strong?!

108. 從後牆外
凝望昔日修院

生查子
成都
1982 年 3 月 8 日

隔牆朝內望，
一角樓房見。
殘破已玻窗，
頂瓦多凌亂。

舊情浮眼前，
後事難研判。
惟願志常存，
不問何年返！

108.   Gazing At Our Old Monastery From Outside The Back Wall

To the Tune of Sheng Zha Zi
(Fresh Berries)
Chengdu
March 8, 1982

Gazing up over the monastery wall,
I see a corner of our building.
Glass windows are broken;
Some tiles on the roof are in disorder.

The old scene appears
Before my eyes;
What will happen
Is not discernible.
I only hope
My ideal is always present here,
No matter
What the year I return!

109. 重訪
蓬安勞改營

訴衷情
蓬安
1982 年 3 月 9 日

離經骨肉恨貞堅，
相處苦難言。
遷居就業申請，
再一次、
赴蓬安。

申請拒，
似春寒，
使心酸。
仰天求主：
「勇氣祈增，
旨意承歡！」

109.   A Revisit
To The Labor-Reform Camp
In Peng'an

To the Tune of Shu Zhong Qing
(Opening One's Hrart)
Peng'an
March 9, 1982

Departing from orthodoxy,
My blood brother hates me,
A loyalist to the true Faith.
It is unspeakable pain for me
To get along with him.
I have come to Peng'an once again
To make application
For moving and employment there.

My application is denied,
This is like the chill of early spring,
Bringing me grief.
I look up to pray to the Lord:
"Strengthen my courage
To do Your Will with joy!"

110. 召注
與中共遂寧縣委
統戰部副部長談話

烏夜啼
遂寧
1982 年 3 月 16 日

早晨應召登門。
問黎君，
不識其人、
名亦未風聞。

教昔捍，
境今蹇，
意明陳。
回答言辭、
錄下以留存。

110.   Called To Interview With The Vice-Director Of The United Front Work Department Of The Suining County Communist Party Committee

To the Tune of Wu Ye Ti
(Crows Cawing at Night)
Suining
March 16, 1982

Called in the morning,
I went to the Department.
I was questioned
About a gentleman, surnamed Li.
In reply,
I do not know this person
Nor have I ever gotten wind of his name.

In former days
I defended the Church;
Today
I am in an awkward situation.
My intention was stated clearly.
My responses were recorded and presereved.

111. 擺攤人行道

生查子
遂寧
1982 年 3 月 21 日

擺攤街道邊，
顧客誠迎迓。
遵意寫書函，
無怠無欺詐。

避兄居鬧街，
詩賦於閒暇；
勤奮日耕耘，
時屆收莊稼！

111. Setting Up
A Stall On The Sidewalk

To the Tune of Sheng Zka Zi
(Fresh Berries)
Suining
March 21, 1982

Setting up a stall
On the edge of the street,
I welcome the clients
With sincerity.
Following their intentions,
I write letters in their behalf,
Without slackness,
Without cheating.

To escape from my brother,
I am now in the busy street.
I can compose my poems at leisure.
If I plough with my pen
Diligently every day,
I will harvest my crops
At the appointed time!

112. 三月二十一日：
為中國教難祈禱日

定風波
遂寧
1982 年 3 月 25 日

善牧離開逼眾羊，
狼仍赤縣逞猖狂。
教難早終羊免禍，
宗座，
要求信友禱穹蒼。

公禱日期今御定，
欣慶，
搏狼戰士志彌昂。
狼盜竟然齊吼叫，
無效，
是非善惡早昭彰！

112.   The March 21st Day, A Day Of Praying For The Persecuted Church In China

To the Tune of Ding Feng Bo
(Calming Storm)
Suining
March 25, 1982

Compelling the sheep
To depart from their Good Shepherd,
The Wolf is still rampant in China.
To put an early end to this persecution,
And to relieve the sheep from this disaster,
The Holy See
Appeals to all the faithful
To pray to Heaven.

The date for the common prayer
Has been now set;
This must elate us,
This will inspire the wolf-wrestling warriors
More high-spirited in battle.
This has also aroused
The roaring of the Wolf and the robbers.
But to no effect,
Because right and wrong, good and evil
Have been made evident long ago!

113. 遂寧香會

菩薩蠻
遂寧
1982 年 4 月

春光三月多明媚，
馳名二廟迎香會。
香客似流川，
遊人如踵連。

燒香巾幗眾，
拜佛青年擁。
禁令效難生，
無神官吏驚！

113.   The Incense Fair In Suining

To the Tune of Pusa Man
(Strange Goddess)
Suining
April 1982

In March
When the two famous temples
Welcome the Joss Stick Fair,
How charming and enchanting,
The scene of the spring light!
Pilgrims come in an endless stream,
And visitors call at the Fair
Following on each other's heels.

Many women burn joss sticks
Before idols;
Young people crowd
To worship the Buddhas.
Seeing their bans failed to go into effect,
The atheist officials are amazed!

114. 復活主日

烏夜啼
遂寧
1982 年 4 月 11 日
復活節

今晨晦暗陰寒，
坐攤邊，
祈禱吟詩、
代客寫書函。

嫈嫈處，
佳節度，
禱皇天：
「**復活**寵恩、
惠注我心田！」

114.   **Easter Sunday**

To the Tune of Wu Ye Ti
(Crows Cawing at Night)
Suining
April 11, 1982
Easter Sunday

This morning
The weather is gloomy and cold.
Sitting on the stall side,
I say prayers,
Or compose poems,
Or write letters for my customers.

All alone,
I celebrate this joyous and holy Festival,
Praying to Heaven:
"Please, Lord, kindly pour
The graces of Your Resurrection
Into my heart!"

115. 欣獲黃國維神父第二次回信

采桑子
遂寧
1982 年 4 月 12 日

年初返梓香江往，
樂敘天倫。
樂敘天倫，
且為傳音與至親。

台兄聞報今猶在，
無比歡欣。
無比歡欣，
去國來朝夢可真！

115.   Joyfully Receiving The Second Reply From Fr. Bernard Huang Guowei

To the Tune of Cai Sang Zi
(Picking Mulberries)
Suining
April 12, 1982

Early this year,
You went back
To your native land,
To Hong Kong.
You had the joys
Of a family living and conversing together.
You had the joys
Of a family living and conversing together,
You also delivered my messages
To my very close relatives.

Hearng from you
That my brother in Taiwan is still living,
I delight without end.
I delight without end,
My dream of leaving the country
Will very likely become a reality some day!

116. 歸家一載

沁園春
遂寧
1982 年 7 月 27 日

鄉別多年，
一載歸來，
仍是舊人。
念鐵窗頑抗，
終歌勝利；
家園奮戰，
正飲酸辛。
蓬勃雄心，
崇高抱負，
一似當初河嶽吞。
全無恨；
蓋常磨劍利，
久煉金純。

難逢志在忠昆，
兩訪錦官城心似焚。
幸良朋西蜀，
傳音急急；

116.   One Year After Homecoming

To the Tune of Qin Yuan Chun
(Spring in the Garden of Qin)
Suining
July 27, 1982

After many years
Of my parting from my native town,
I am still the same person,
When I came back one year ago.
In the past,
Through a strenuous fight behind prison bars,
I sang a triumphant song at last.
Now,
In the vigorous battle in the homeland,
I am drinking the bitterness.
My lofty aspiration and my high ideals
Can conquer rivers and mountains,
Just as in the beginning.
I have no regret at all:
The sword can be much sharper
Through constant grinding,
And the gold can be much purer
Through long refining.

It is difficult to find
The old loyal brothers
Remaining faithful still;
My heart was burning with anxiety
During my two visits to Chengdu.
Fortunately,
My good friends in west Sichuan
Delivered my messages very fast,

賢師東海，
施惠頻頻。
既解身窮，
復增豪氣，
鏤骨銘肌天父恩。
春暉沐，
定高歌慈愛，
勇搏蛇神！

And my worthy teachers across the eastern seas
Bestowed on me their favors again and again.
Thus,
My physical destitution was relieved,
And my morale was heightened.
Their favors,
Considered as the kindness of the Heavenly Father,
Are engraved on my bones and heart.
Bathed in the spring sunlight,
I will surely sing with a loud voice
The Father's loving-kindness
And battle with an unyielding courage
With the snake demons!

117. 電影《少林寺》
觀後

七絕
遂寧
1982 年 8 月 1 日

禍國殃民煬帝狂，
率師討伐李淵昂。
少林僧侶同仇愾，
除暴聲名望再揚！

117. After Watching The Movie *Shaolin Si*

In the Poetic Style of Qijue
Suining
August 1, 1982

Bringing disaster to the country,
And carryng calamity to the people,
The Emperor Yang was a maniac.
Li Yuan commanded
With high morale
A punitive army against him.
The Buddhist monks of the Shsolin Temple
Shared a bitter hatred
Of the same enemy;
Their reputation
Of having removed the tyranny
Is expected to be made known
Once again in the present time!

118. 廣德寺觀音會

水龍吟
遂寧
1982 年 8 月 8 日

立秋時節天炎，
慶登蓮座觀音母。
燒香頂禮，
蜂擁而至，
善男信女。
廣德西郊，
人山人海，
騰騰煙霧。
竟昔年情景，
今朝再現，
心黎庶，
歸何處？

被佔遭焚廟宇，
殆難尋、
舊時風度。
浮屠坡石，

118.   The Guanyin (Goddess Of Mercy) Fair In The Guangde Temple

To the Tune of Shui Long Yin
(The Water Dragon Howling)
Suining
August 8, 1982

At the beginning of autumn,
In a season still hot,
The Goddess of Mercy is celebrated
As she mounts the Lotus Seat.
To burn joss sticks,
To pay homage,
Buddhist devotees,
Good men and believing women,
Come swarming there.
The Guangde Temple in the western suburbs
Is a sea of people.
It is filled with an endless stream of smoke.
Unexpectedly,
The scenes of those years reappear today!
The hearts of the people,
Where are they turning now?

This temple once suffered
Occupation and fire.
Its original form
Is hard to discover.
Its towers, rocks on the hilldide,

劫餘殘跡，
亦蒙光顧。
週末良辰，
遊客信眾，
熙來攘去。
睹斯情此景，
且憂且恨，
反神官府！

Even its traces and signs
Remaining from the calamity,
All of these are also patronized.
At the weekends,
On good and bright days,
Tourists and Buddhists frequent there,
Coming and going in crowds.
Seeing this scene,
Facing this sight,
The godless authorities
Are both anxious and hateful!

119. 聖母升天慶節有感

昭君怨
遂寧
1982 年 8 月 15 日

玉體升天神妙，
震古鑠今榮耀。
卅載信條頌，
慶年年。

猶見**紅旗**飄舞，
兒女滿腔愁緒。
舉國頌**春暉**，
在何時？

119.   Impressions On The Solemnity Of The Assumption Of The Blessed Virgin Mary

To the Tune of Zhao Jun Yuan
(The Complaint of Zhao Jun)
Suining
August 15, 1982

O Saint Mary,
Our loving Mother,
Your jade body ascended into Heaven
In a wonderful way.
Your glory astonished the ancient ages
And amazed the modern world.
Proclaimed for thirty years,
This dogma has been celebrated
Year after year.

Seeing still the Red flag flapping and dancing,
Your Chinese children are weighed down
With anxieties.
The whole nation will praise
Your motherly kindness as the light of spring,
At what time?

120. 生日述懷

憶王孫
遂寧
1982 年 8 月 26 日

由蓉返里卅年前，
自獄今歸一暑寒。
窘境兩朝志悉堅。
望餘年，
霜雪務教華髮妍！

120.   **Pouring Out My Heart On My Birthday**

To the Tune of Yi Wang Sun
(Thinking of Wang Sun)
Suining
August 26, 1982

Thirty years ago
I came back from Chengdu;
Today,
I have returned from a jail
For a summer and a winter.
In these two sorry plights
My will has been always steadfast.
During my remaining years
I hope:
Frost and snow will make
My white hair splendid!

121. 看電影
《新天方夜譚》

七絕
遂寧
1982 年 8 月 27 日

哈桑壯志滿胸膛，
採得玫瑰除惡王。
故事天方傳已久，
期望重演在東方！

121.   Watching The Movie
The New Tales
Of The Arabian Nights

In the Poetic Style of Qijue
Suining
August 27, 1982

Filled with lofty ambitions,
Hasan succeeded
In picking the roses
And in wiping out the evil monarch.
This Arabian story has been spread
Over a long, long time.
Its recurrence is awaited
In the East today!

122. 哀悼
遭中共處決的
五位劫機人員

減字木蘭花
遂寧
1982 年 9 月

垂成君敗，
被捕受刑遭殺害。
同道芸芸，
亦受株連進獄門。

獻台機密，
棄共劫機非可斥。
痛悼英靈，
求主惠然賜永生！

122.   Mourning For The Execution Of The Five Hijackers By The Chinese Communists

To the Tune of Jian Zi Mulan Hua
(The Magnolia)
Suining
September 1982

You suffered defeat
When victory was within your grasp.
You were arrested, tortured and killed.
Many of your companions with the same ideals
Were also implicated and thrown in jail.

To offer to Taiwan their classified secrets,
You abandoned the Communists
And hijacked the airliner.
Your action should not be rebuked.
Grieving deeply over you, O heroic souls,
We pray to the gracious Lord
For your eternal life!

123. 獲台灣五哥
責難信

鷓鴣天
遂寧
1982 年 9 月 26 日

字跡親情一若前，
信函五頁震心弦。
嚴詞譴責非公允，
盛意關懷卻顯然。

離北國，
往南天，
魂勞夢斷好多年。
除非離境援將絕，
聞訊心疼似匕穿！

123.   Receiving A Blaming Letter From My Fifth-Elder Brother Philip In Taiwan

To the Tune of Zhegu Tian
(Partridges in the Sky)
Suining
September 26, 1982

Your handwriting and intimacy
Are just as before;
Your five-page letter
Shook my heart strings.
Your blame in strong words
May not be just and fair,
But your concern from a great kindness
Is clear.

Departing from the North
And going to the South,
This have I thought of, envisioned,
Imagined and dreamed of
For so many, many years.
Your help will be broken off
Unless I am allowed to leave the country.
Hearing of the message such as this,
My heart feels pained
As if being stabbed with a dagger!

124. 中秋節

蘇幕遮
遂寧
1982 年 10 月 1 日

雨晨霏，
陰午轉，
八角巍亭，
登上天將晚。
蕭瑟秋風來拂面，
燈火萬家，
景色真輝燦。

境淒涼，
胸悶倦，
前景茫茫，
何日方明顯？
萬緒千情心繚亂。
雲破月來，
祝願**貞娘**獻！

124.   **The Mid-Autumn Festival**

To the Tune of Su Mu Zhe
(The Felt Hat)
Suining
October 1, 1982

Rain in the morning,
Overcast from midday;
When evening is drawing near
I mount the towering Octagonal Pavilion.
There the autumn wind is murmuring,
Stroking my face.
Myriad twinkling lights of the city
Create a truly brilliant sight.

My plight is desolate,
My heart is bored and listless.
When will my prospects
Turn from bleak to clear?
Filled with countless feelings,
My heart is complicated and confused.
Suddenly,
The clouds break,
And the moon appears.
I offer my wishes
To the Blessed Virgin Mother!

125. 聖五傷方濟各
誕辰八百週年
紀念郵票

七絕
遂寧
1983 年 1 月 15 日

救人頌主語鏗鏘，
好鳥枝頭洗耳聆。
頭上髮圈光四放，
全球普照潤心靈！

125.   The Commemorative Stamp Of The Eight Hundredth Anniversary Birthday Of Saint Francis With The Stigmata

In the Poetic Style of Qijue
Suining
January 15, 1983

Your words, O Saint Francis,
For saving men and praising the Lord,
Are so full of resonance
That beloved birds on the branches
Are listening
With respectful attention.
The tonsure of your head
Sheds its rays in all directions,
Illumining the whole world,
Moistening hearts and minds!

126. 悼吳伯皋同學

人月圓
遂寧
1983 年 2 月 9 日

神州變色君驚恐，
順水以推舟。
三年短促，
官場未進，
卻入墳丘！

蒙邀合影，
誼如金石，
同學三秋。
重逢吾惘，
天堂君望，
向主恭求！

126.   Lamenting The Death Of Wu Bogao, My Schoolmate

To the Tune of Ren Yue Yuan
(The Family Reunion and the Full Moon)
Suining
February 9, 1983

When China, our Divine Land,
Changed her political color
You were terrified.
You were to
Push Your boat along with the current.
During the last three years,
A very short period,
You have not yet entered
The ranks of officialdom,
You instead went to the grave!

You had once invited me
To have a joint photo taken,
Showing our friendship
As firm as metal and stone.
We were schoolmates for three autumns.
I was disappointed at our recent reunions.
For the Paradise you were yearning for
I pray reverently to the Lord!

127. 春節除夕

七絕
遂寧
1983 年 2 月 12 日

家家門柱赤春聯，
爆竹轟鳴震九天。
歡聚鄰居聞笑語，
何年修院慶團圓？

127.   The Spring Festival's Eve

In the Poetic Style of Qijue
Suining
February 12, 1983

On the gateposts of every house
There are red Spring Festival couplets.
Firecrackers go off,
Thundering so loudly
Enough to shake the firmament.
I hear the laughing and the talk
From the happily reunited neighbors.
In what year
Will my monastic family
Celebrate its reunion?

128. 喜得
唐天壽神父回信

七絕
遂寧
1983 年 5 月

正愁好雁幾時還，
今現眼前開笑顏。
一片丹心天父動：
東西通道暢如前。

128.   Rejoicing
In Receiving A Reply
From Fr. Felix Tang Tianshou

In the Poetic Style of Qjiue
Suining
May 1983

While worrying about
When the beloved goose
Will bring back to me a reply,
I see it appear today before my eyes,
Beaming with joy.
My loyal heart has moved
Our Heavenly Father:
The passage between East and West
Is easy and smooth
As in the past.

129. 題贈唐天壽神父
《星彔小楷字帖》

蝶戀花
遂寧
1983 年 5 月 14 日

舊夢當年《星彔》喚，
四十年前情景今重現。
假日臨摹從未斷，
功深筆力真雄健。

懷念暮雲春樹看，
三獲華箋慶幸愁眉展。
字帖騰空飛彼岸，
來朝抵掌談歡忭！

129.   Dedication On The *Xinglu Xiaokai Zitie*
(Xinglu Copybook In Small Characters)
To Fr. Felix Tang Tianshou

To the Tune of Die Lian Hua
(Butterflies Courting Flowers)
Suining
May 14, 1983

The "Xinglu" evokes
My former dreams of those years;
The scene of forty years before
Reappears at present.
On holidays,
You, Fr. Felix, used to practicise
Calligraphy after this model without ceasing.
Because of your constant and effective practicising,
The strokes of your calligraphy
Were really powerful.

Looking at these spring trees,
I call to mind
Those evening clouds of your place.
Having received your esteemed letters
Three times,
I rejoiced and my worried brows unknitted.
Now,
This copybook rises to the sky,
And flies to the other shore.
I hope we will chat one day
With clapping hands,
Unconstrained, free and joyous!

130. 題五舅母遺照

七律
遂寧
1983 年 6 月 22 日

兒時隨母謁慈顏，
別夢依稀五十年。
長壽安寧曾享受，
伶仃孤苦亦糾纏！
人間逆旅應辭別，
天上家園慶返還。
凝視遺容思往景，
重逢神國望來天！

130.   Inscription On The Photograph Of My deceased Fifth Aunt

In the Poetic Style of Qilu
Suining
June 22, 1983

In my childhood,
I followed my mother
To visit you, Oh, my fifth aunt!
The vague dream of parting
Passed away for fifty years.
You enjoyed longevity and tranquility,
But you were also bothered
In a forlorn and alone plight!
You should depart the earthly inn,
And happily return to the Heavenly home.
Staring at your face on the photo,
I remember the past scene.
I hope to see you again
Some day in the Divine Kingdom!

131. 題詞於 與雙親的合照

四言詩
遂寧
1983 年 6 月 22 日

母離人間，三十三年；
八載之後，父亦歸天。

合影一幀，卅七年前；
慈容今睹，樂也陶然。

春暉深厚，何以銜環？
續衛**聖教**，奮戰狂瀾！

131. Inscription On The Group Photo With My Parents

In the Poetic Style of Siyan Shi
Suining
June 22, 1983

My mother parted from this world
Thirty-three years ago.
Eight years later,
My father returned to God.

Thirty-seven years ago,
A group photo was taken with them.
Looking now at their loving faces,
I am cheerful.

For their profound kindnesses—
Their sunshine of spring,
How am I to repay?
Defending continuously the Holy Church,
Fighting bravely the raging waves!

132.　歸家兩年

三言詩
遂寧
1983 年 7 月 27 日

凱歌唱，還鄉梓。
兄異趣，戰重啟。

艱險境，剛強志；
迎挑釁，鼓勇氣，

鴿奉派，信傳遞；
歸來時，回音至。

郎師邀，往蓉市；
知原院，獲助喜。

兄海外，賜指示；
希望增，去國事。

境改善，須再勵；
恃主佑，奪勝利！

132.   Back Home For Two Years

In the Poetic Style of Sanyan Shi
Suining
July 27, 1983

Singing a triumphant song,
I came back home.
In virtue of my brother's different interest,
I was bound to resume the struggle.

My plight is hard and dangerous,
But my will is firm and unyielding.
Meeting head-on the provocations,
I pluck up my courage.

Having been dispatched,
My pigeon delivered the letter.
On return,
It brought back to me a reply.

At the invitation of Professor Pansy Lang,
I went to the city of Chengdu;
I was informed of my original monastery
And took delight in obtaining help from it.

My overseas brother
Gave me instructions;
My hope of leaving the country
Is increasing.

My situation has improved,
And I should continue exerting myself.
Relying on the Lord's assistance,
I strive for the victory!

133. 緬懷唐天壽神父

清平樂
遂寧
1983 年 9 月 21 日

兼年轉瞬，
幾度通音信。
蒙受恩情心振奮，
謝意一言難盡！

當今天各一方，
中橫浩瀚汪洋。
跨海聯歡誰助？
抬頭祈禱穹蒼！

133.   Thinking Of Fr. Felix Tang Tianshou

To the Tune of Qing Ping Yue
(The Qing Ping Song)
Suining
September 21, 1983

During the last two years,
As if in a flash,
We have communicated with each other
Several times.
Greatly favored by you,
I have been inspired and heartened up.
My gratitude is hard to express
In a few words!

At present,
We are far apart from each other.
Between us
There is a vast and mighty ocean.
Who is able
To help me leap across the sea
To have a get-together with you?
Raising my head,
I pray to Heaven!

134. 思念黃國維神父

七律
遂寧
1983 年 9 月 21 日

同居共處四秋歡，
離別卅春滿苦酸。
常憶音容心儘喜，
久違教誨意難安。
姍姍鴻雁終來到，
滾滾波濤枉阻攔。
景色西山依舊在，
同遊攜手在何天？

134.   Remembering Fr. Bernard Huang Guowei

In the Poetic Style of Qilu
Suining
September 21, 1983

I rejoiced,
Living with you
For four autumns;
But I grieved
Over our separation
Of forty springs.
Recalling often your voice and countenance,
I am happy;
Missing your instructions for ages,
I feel uneasy.
Your letter, as a swan goose, slow in coming,
Arrived to me finally,
Breaking through
The vain arrest of the surging waves.
The scenery of Xishan
Remained unchanged;
On what day
Will we go sightseeing hand in hand?

135. 驚悉
昔日兩位老神學生
蒲通華先生和張順明先生
將由愛國會主教祝聖爲神父

四言詩
遂寧
1983 年 12 月 1 日

三十三年，**紅旗**飄蕩；
教區神父，早隨搖晃。

己已耄耋，需人接棒；
覓得二人，年邁身壯。

昔神學生，極易培養；
五月功成，晉鐸在望。

聖誕節前，非黨意向；
改期指令，突從天降！

延期再議，令眾沮喪；
「自治自傳」，哀哉尚饗！

135. A Surprise To Learn Two Old Former Theologians, Mr. Pu Tonghua And Mr. Zhang Shunming, Will Be Ordained To The Priesthood By A Patriotic Bishop

In the Poetic Style of Siyan Shi
Suining
December 1, 1983

For thirty-three years,
Since the Red flag began to flap,
The priests of this diocese
Have long been swaying with it.

Already octogenarians themselves,
They need others to succeed.
Two men have been found;
These two, aged but strong.

Moreover, being old theologians,
They can be trained very easily.
They have obtained good results
From the five-month training.
They are hopeful
About the priestly ordination.

The date before Christmas
Is not the intention of the Party.
An order of changing the date
Comes down from heaven unexpectedly!

The delay and the rediscussion
Make all of them depressed!
Alas!
Oh, Self-administration and Self-propagation,
May you enjoy this!

136. 1984 年元旦

烏夜啼
遂寧
1984 年 1 月 1 日

迎來佳節冬陽，
喜洋洋。
經濟振興、
景氣現城鄉。

控信仰，
箝思想，
惜如常！
花朵自由、
何日吐芬芳？

136.   New Year's Day, 1984

To the Tune of Wu Ye Ti
(Crows Cawing at Night)
Suining
January 1, 1984

Welcoming the happy festival
Under a winter sun,
I beam with joy.
Since the economy has been vitalized,
There is a boom
In cities and the countryside.

Faith is controlled,
Thoughts are gagged.
All this,
Pitifully,
Is as usual!
The flower of freedom,
On what day
Will it burst its fragrance?

137. 向城關公安派出所
遞交出國申請書

鵲橋仙
遂寧
1984 年 1 月 23 日

艱難處境，
忠貞肝膽，
衛**教**立場如故。
深思遠景細籌謀，
亦奮戰、
毒**蛇猛虎**。

多回通信，
長期思考，
準備安排就緒。
今交申請與官方，
出國事、
由茲上路！

137.   Presenting My Exit Petition To The Chengguan Police Station

To the Tune of Que Qiao Xian
(The Magpie Bridge)
Suining
January 23, 1984

Despite in a sorry plight,
I remain loyal.
My position of defending the Church
Is the same as before.
I have deeply thought of my prospects
And carefully made plans,
While bravely fighting
Against the venomous Snake and the fierce Tiger.

After many correspondences
And protracted considerations,
The preparations and arrangements are complete.
Now,
I present my application to the authorites.
Thus,
The matter of my going abroad
Sets out on a journey!

138. 春節全家福

七絕
遂寧
1984 年 2 月 3 日

爆竹一鳴萬象新，
團圓闔宅喜迎春。
全家合影長留念，
何在來春問此身？

138.   Family Photo
Taken At The Spring Festival

In the Poetic Style of Qijue
Suining
February 3, 1984

Along with the blast
Of the going-off firecracker,
Everything looks fresh and joyful.
My reunited family exults
At welcoming the spring.
A family photo has been taken
As a permanent memento.
I ask myself:
Where will I be
Next spring?

139. 題贈
十二歲姪外孫女蔣雲
《現代漢語小詞典》

七絕
遂寧
1984 年 2 月 3 日

知識無涯似海洋，
富藏珍寶好風光。
扁舟一葉雄心樹，
尋寶探幽立起航！

139.   Dedication In The *Small Modern Chinese Dictionary* To Jiang Yun, My Grandniece At Age 12

In the Poetic Style of Qijue
Suining
February 3, 1984

Knowledge is
As boundless as an ocean.
Rich in jewels and valuables,
It has a wonderful sight.
You,
Jiang Yun,
As a small boat,
Should,
With lofty ideals,
Right now, quickly set sail
To seek treasures
And to search for secrets!

140. 出國申請
已轉交給縣公安局

如夢令
遂寧
1984 年 2 月 24 日

申請四週呈遞，
已轉上峰知喜。
小鳥錮多年，
飛出鐵籠希冀。
希冀，
希冀，
宿願合乎天意！

140.   My Petition For Leaving The Country Already Forwarded To The County Public Security Bureau

To the Tune of Ru Meng Ling
(Like a Dream)
Suining
February 24, 1984

Submitted four weeks ago,
My petition has been forwarded
To the authorities.
I delighted in learning this.
As a small bird,
Confined for many years,
I hoped
For flying out of the iron cage.
Hoping,
Hoping,
My long-cherished wish
Will conform with the Will of Heaven!

141. 三訪郎毓秀教授

點絳脣
遂寧
1984 年 3 月 8 日

一月春寒，
如油細雨征程浥。
卅年民襲，
猶未淒風息。

鐵幕思離，
星火心情急。
奔蓉邑，
疑難胸臆，
懇請郎師釋。

141.   My Third Visit To Professor Pansy Lang Yuxiu

To the Tune of Dian Jiang Chun
(Rouged Lips)
Suining
March 8, 1984

The chill of early spring
Lasts one month.
Fine rain,
As precious as oil,
Moistens my way.
Having made inroads on the people,
The cold wind has not yet subsided.

Thinking of leaving the Iron Curtain,
I am in a worried and impatient mood.
I am going to the city of Chengdu,
For the purpose
Of requesting earnestly Professor Lang
To remove some doubts and difficulties
From my heart.

142. 自蓉回遂途中

七律
成都
1984 年 3 月 18 日

消除疑慮恩師別，
撒滿朝霞路返鄉。
樹木行人拋後面，
豪情壯志向前方。
休嫌旋里蒙塵垢，
確信凌空越海洋。
主乃萬能慈善父，
未來絢麗似春光！

142.   On My Way Back To Suining From Chengdu

In the Poetic Style Of Qilu
Chengdu
March 18, 1984

Having dispelled my misgivings,
I take leave of my esteemed professor.
The rosy dawn sprays its light
On my way back to my native place.
Trees and passers-by
Are left behind,
My lofty sentiments and aspirations
Keep on moving forward.
I should not complain
Of suffering dust and dirt
While going back home;
But be sure
That I will soar aloft
And cut across seas and oceans.
The Lord is
Almighty, merciful and loving Father;
My future will be as brilliant
As the spring light!

143. 愛國會
黃渥澤神父的警訊

破陣子
遂寧
1984 年 4 月 18 日

「新教南充二牧，
寄函國外遭關。
宜勸爾家頑固弟，
海外關聯立斷完，
消災身可安！」

緊要非常黃訊，
嫂今暗地來傳。
愁懼音容令我痛。
聽勸豈當以苟全?!
捶胸問昊天?!

143.   An Alarming Message From Fr. HuangWoze, The Patriotic Priest

To the Tune of Po Zhen Zi
(Storming the Enemy's Position)
Suining
April 18, 1984

"**T**wo Protestant pastors in Nanchong
Have been put behind bars
For sending letters abroad.
You need to persuade
That obstinate brother in your family
To cut off at once
All his overseas relationships.
Thus,
He may avoid a disaster
And keep his body safe!"

This extremely critical message from Fr. Huang
My sister-in-law comes today
To deliver me in secret.
The worried and fearful expression
On her face and in her voice
Distresses me very much.
To save my skin,
Should I comply with their advice?!
Beating my breast,
I appeal to Heaven?!

144. 聞黃渥澤神父
要求縣宗教事務科新科長
處理我的問題

卜算子
遂寧
1984 年 7 月 25 日

山頂挺**蒼松**，
勇鬥風霜雨。
三十餘年百戰翁，
翠潔仍如故。

枯樹麓呻吟，
松望羞成怒。
縱得狂飆雪恨仇，
松碧將彌著！

144. Hearing Of Fr. Huang Woze's Request Raised To The New Head Of The County Religious Affairs Bureau To Handle My Matter

To the Tune of Pu Suan Zi
(The Fortune Teller)
Suining
July 25, 1984

Standing erect on the top of the hill,
The green pine has combated bravely
Against wind, frost and rain.
More than thirty years later,
Now,
An old one undergoing a hundred battles,
It remains green and pure
As before.

On the foot of the hill
A withered tree groans.
Looking up at the pine,
It is shamed into anger.
Even if successfully beckoning
A hurricane to wreak vengeance,
It can only make
The pine's jade face more remarkable!

145. 題照惜別
黃自扶好友

醜奴兒
遂寧
1984 年 9 月 28 日

兒時相遇難相語。
重晤蓉城；
藝校姿英，
預測前程如日昇。

多年繫獄嘗酸苦，
少展才能。
種種離情，
彩筆祈揮入畫屏！

145.   Dedication On A Photo
To Bidding Farewell
To Mr. Huang Zifu, A Good Friend

To the Tune of Chou Nu Er
(The Ugly Slave)
Suining
September 28, 1984

During our boyhood,
When we occasionally met,
We scarcely talked to each other.
When we met again
In the city of Chengdu,
I saw you with a talented bearing,
You then,
A student in
The Sichuan Provincial Academy of Fine Arts.
I presupposed your prospects
Being as brilliant as the rising sun.

Imprisoned for many years,
You tasted bitterness and pains.
You have shown to the public, in a limited way,
Your talents and abilities.
A variety of the parting feelings,
I would ask you,
To wield your colored bruth
To put onto a painted screen!

146. 題照贈別好友 蕭莉琨女士

搗練子
遂寧
1984 年 9 月 28 日

如陌路，
昔相逢。
荊識還鄉樂五中。
才藝壯懷堪讚賞，
感恩辭別禱蒼穹。

146. Dedication On A Photo At Parting To A Good Friend, Ms. Xiao Likun

To the Tune of Dao Lian Zi
(Pounding Silk Floss)
Suining
September 28, 1984

We looked like strangers,
When we came across in the past.
On my return to the hometown,
I was very glad
To get the honor
Of making your acquaintance.
Your artistic talents and lofty aspirations
Are worthy of appreciations.
To express my gratitude,
To say goodbye,
I pray to Heaven for you!

147. 題贈慕道新友 李劍農先生 新聖經一冊

清平樂
遂寧
1984 年 9 月 29 日

耶穌慈主，
救世生於婦。
傳道驅魔祛病苦，
釘死**歸天**道佈。

新經記**主**生平，
恩真善智充盈。
常讀深思力踐，
善終享福**天庭**！

147.   Dedication On A Copy Of The New Testament To Mr. Li Jiannong, A New Friend Who Longs For The Truth

To the Tune of Qing Ping Yue
(The Qing Ping Song)
Suining
September 29, 1984

Jesus, our merciful Lord,
Was born of woman
To save the world.
He preached His doctrines,
He exorcised devils,
He dispelled diseases and pains.
When He was crucified
And returned to Heaven,
His doctrines began to propagate.

The New Testament records the life of the Lord,
Filled with graces, truth, goodness and wisdom.
Through always reading,
Deeply thinking and vigorously practicing,
We will have a good death
And enjoy happiness in the Heavenly court!

148. 題照贈別
李張兩位醫生

憶江南
遂寧
1984 年 10 月 3 日

相識短，
情誼厚而深。
設宴餞行蒙盛意；
題詞小照自衷心，
敬獻表微忱。

148.   Dedication On A Photo To Say Goodbye To Doctor Li And Doctor Zhang

To the Tune of Yi Jiang Nan
(Remembering the South of the River)
Suining
October 3, 1984

I made your acquaintance
Only a short time ago.
Our friendship is deep.
I am favored
With a farewell banquet in my honor.
The dedication and the photo,
With my sincere heart,
I offer to you respectfully
As a humble token of my gratitude.

149. 題書贈老中醫
柴煥章先生

憶秦娥
遂寧
1984 年 10 月 4 日

南冠摘，
歸家成豆箕煎急。
箕煎急，
舊憂剛釋，
新愁來襲！

兩年相識西街側，
承蒙關照煢煢客。
煢煢客，
感恩辭別，
獻書一冊！

149.   Dedication On A Book To Mr. Cai Huanzhang, An Old Chinese Doctor

To the Tune of Yi Qin E
(Remenbering the Beauty of Qin)
Suining
October 4, 1984

With the prisoner's "hat" removed,
I retruned home.
Soon thereafter
I became beans
Cooked violently by the beanstalks.
Cooked violently by the beanstalks,
I was just set free from the old sorrows,
But immediately attacked by the new griefs!

By the side of West Street,
We have made acquaintance
For two years.
You have shown your concern
For me,
A lonely man.
A lonely man,
Bidding farewell with gratitude,
I offer you this book!

150. 題照贈新
友李劍農先生

眼兒媚
遂寧
1984 年 10 月 4 日

擺攤前載大街邊，
相遇有機緣，
退休不久，
頻繁路過，
時或交談。

親朋協助將離境，
脫困謝蒼天！
臨行祝願：
信從上主，
得救欣歡！

150.   Dedication On A Photo
To Mr. Li Jiannong, A New Friend

To the Tune of Yan Er Mei
(The Eyes' Fascination)
Suining
October 4, 1984

The year before last,
When I set up a stall
On the sidewalk of the great street,
I had a good chance to meet you.
Retired before long,
You often passed by
And at times talked with me.

With the help of my relatives and friends,
I am about to leave the country.
Freeing myself from the awkward plight,
I am grateful to Heaven!
On departure,
I wish
You would believe in the Lord,
Be saved and exult!

151. 題照贈別
姨孃王淑漢

生查子
遂寧
1984 年 10 月 4 日

外公亡果州，
嘗與扶靈柩，
由是識尊顏
今晤卅年後。

育童多載更，
髮白容彌皺。
臨別有何望？
來日天堂覯！

151.   Dedication On A Photo To Say Goodbye To My Aunt, Wang Shuhan

To the Tune of Sheng Zha Zi
(Fresh Berries)
Suining
October 4, 1984

When my maternal grandfather died
In Guozhou (Nanchong Xian),
I escorted the hearse
Together with you, my aunt.
Thus,
I knew you by sight.
Today,
Forty years later,
I see you again.

Having raised schoolboys
For many years,
Your hair became white,
Your face, wrinkly.
At this parting,
Whar is my hope?
One day,
We will meet in Paradise!

152. 題照
謝好友黃自扶先生
五幅水彩畫

西江月
遂寧
1984 年 10 月 5 日

三載歸來窘陷，
無顏舊誼重溫。
光明景現逐愁雲，
往報佳音興奮。

巧奪天工彩畫，
題詞字秀情真。
來朝重晤在何春？
佳作伴隨休恨！

152.   Dedication On A Photo In Thanksgiving To Mr. Huang Zifu, A Good Friend, For His Five Watercolor Paintings

To the Tune of Xi Jiang Yue
(Moon over the West River)
Suining
October 5, 1984

Since my return,
I have been cornered
For three years.
I did not have the face
To revive our old friendship.
Now,
A brilliant scene appears to me
And dispels the gloomy clouds.
I am excited
To bring to you the good news.

Your watercolor paintings.
Are wonderful handiwork rivaling nature.
Your inscriptions
Are beautiful and sincere.
In which spring
Will we meet again
Some day in the future?
In the company
Of your excellent paintings,
I should not regret!

153. 悼黃自輝神父

人月圓
遂寧
1984 年 10 月 6 日

摔傷去載今辭世，
聞訊不勝憂。
西山共處，
遂寧重晤、
憶往增愁。

神州濤湧，
漁舟搖晃、
公逐潮流。
尊軀入墓，
公魂為救，
向主哀求！

153.   Mourning For Fr. Huang Zihui

To the Tune of Ren Yue Yuan
(The Family Reunion and the Full Moon)
Suining
October 6, 1984

You, Fr. Huang,
Fell down and injured yourself last year;
You now departed the world.
Upon hearing the news,
I am laden with great sorrow.
We lived together once in Xishan,
We met again in Suining:
Recalling the past,
I deepen my sadness.

When in China, in the Divine Land,
The great waves began to roar
And the Fishing Boat began to rock,
You drifted with the tide.
Now,
Your body has gone down
To the grave.
For the salvation of your soul,
I am piteously entreat the Lord!

154. 告別遂寧

醜奴兒
遂寧
1984 年 10 月 7 日

東方欲曉兄家別，
舒暢心身。
前往東門，
乘上班車蓉市奔。

三年戰役終於勝，
深謝天恩！
鄉梓離欣，
前景輝煌似彩雲！

154. **Bidding Farewell To Suining**

To the Tune of Chou Nu Er
(The Ugly Slave)
Suining
October 7, 1984

When dawn breaks in the East,
I leave my brother's family,
Happy in mind and body.
I go to the east gate
To ride in a long-distance bus
To the city of Chengdu.

I have won the three-year battle,
I am deeply grateful
To the favor of Heaven.
I take delight
In leaving the home town.
My prospects display themselves
As splendid as color clouds!

155. 路過簡陽
思念法籍堂區主任
甘神父

憶江南
簡陽
1984 年 10 月 7 日

思往事，
三十五年前。
暑假隨華甘牧訪，
堂區作客月餘歡。
為主後遭關。

155.   While Passing Through Jianyang, I Think Of Fr. Gazett, A French Pastor

To the Tune of Yi Jiang Nan
(Remembering the South of the River)
Jianyang
October 7, 1984

I think of the past events
Thirty-five years ago.
During the summer vacation,
We followed Fr. Eleutherius Winance
To visit Fr. Gazett.
We felt very happy
To be guests in his parish
For more than one month.
He was imprisoned later
For the Lord.

156. 題照告別尊長
蕭濟醫生和郎毓秀教授

菩薩蠻
成都
1984 年 10 月 8 日

炎炎酷暑滂沱掃，
舊窠將返籠中鳥。
四度扣尊門，
叨光承教欣。

秋光**西岸**朗，
展翅今飛往。
臨別斷愁腸，
重逢**天上**鄉！

156.   Dedication On A Photo To Bid Farewell To My Elders And Betters, Dr. Michel Xiao Ji And Professor Pansy Lang Yuxiu

To the Tune of Pusa Man
(Strange Goddess)
Chengdu
October 8, 1984

The scorching, sweltering heat of summer
Has been wiped out by a torrential rain.
The bird in a cage
Will be returning to its old nest.
I knocked at your door four times;
I am very joyful
To have been favored
With your kindness and instructions.

The autumn scene on the Western Seacoast
Is bright;
Now I get ready for flight there.
Departing from you,
I am heartbroken,
With a hope
That we will meet again
In the Heavenly home!

157. 訪銀大娘未遂

憶江南
成都
1984 年 10 月 9 日

門鎖住，
兩度訪無功。
未見笑容誠憾事；
憶君**教難**拒卑躬，
天上望重逢！

157.   A Visit To Aunt Yin In Vain

To the Tune of Yi Jiang Nan
(Remembering the South of the River)
Chengdu
October 9, 1984

The door is locked,
I visit you twice in vain.
It is truly a pity
That I missed your smiling face.
I call on mind
Your refusal to lower your horn
During the religious persecution.
I hope
We will reunite in Heaven!

158. 告別
應嘉元和蕭柏伉儷

七絕
成都
1984 年 10 月 10 日

臨行辭別上尊門，
小照祈交父母親。
囑託存胸當力辦，
期望願遂沐天恩！

158.   Saying Goodbye
To Married Couple,
Ying Jiayuan And Xiao Bai

In the Poetic Style of Qijue
Chengdu
October 10, 1984

On my departure,
I visit you
To bid farewell
And to beseech you
To pass on a small ptoto to your parents.
Your charge is kept in my mind
And will be handled to my best.
I hope
That you will achieve your wishes
And receive favor
From Heaven!

159. 遊故宮

七絕
北京
1984 年 10 月 14 日

五百多年宮屹昂，
輝煌畫棟與雕梁。
豪華宮殿終生寓，
功德流芳幾帝王？

159.   A Stroll In Gugong (The Imperial Palace)

In the Poetic Style of Qijue
Beijing
October 14, 1984

The palace has stood exalted
Like a giant
For over five hundred years.
Its painted rafters and carved beams
Remain splendid, brilliant.
The emperors lived
In this luxurious palace
All their lives.
How many of them
Have left behind
The fragrances of their merits and virtues?

160. 遊覽
明十三陵
和十三陵水庫

七絕
北京
1984 年 10 月 15 日

營建宏陵御體埋，
死生諸帝耗民財！
修成水庫念餘載，
驚見全枯誠可哀！

160. Sightseeing The Ming Shisanling (The Ming Tombs) And The Shisanling Reservoir

In the Poetic Style of Qijue
Beijing
October 15, 1984

Having built magnificent tombs
To bury their imperial bodies,
The emperors spent great wealth of the people
During their lives
As well as
After their death!
The reservoir was constructed
Over twenty years;
It is a real pity
To be shocked
To see it totally dried up!

161. 路過
毛主席紀念堂

憶江南
北京
1984 年 10 月 15 日

金字匾，
廊柱石花崗；
金瓦琉璃光閃閃，
殿堂宏偉又軒昂！
毛豈永名揚?!

161.   Passing By The Chairman Mao Memorial Hall

To the Tune of Yi Jiang Nan
(Remembering the South of the River)
Beijing
October 15, 1984

With gold-inscribed board,
With granitic corridors,
With glittering golden glazed tiles,
The hall is magnificent and impressive!
Can this hall make Mao
Win an eternal renown?!

162. 觀光
頤和園（夏宮）

七絕
北京
1984 年 10 月 23 日

亭廊堂殿已斑斕，
園塔湖山復壯觀。
帝建遊園黎庶苦，
遊人觀賞卻欣然！

162.   Seeing The Sights Of Yiheyuan (The Summer Palace)

In the Poetic Style of Qijue
Beijing
October 23, 1984

Pavilions, corridors, temples and halls
Are gorgeous;
Gardens, pagodas, lakes and hills
Are also magnificent.
In constructing the park for amusement,
The emperors brought sufferings to the people.
Yet,
Tourists delight in enjoying the sight!

163. 北京大學

七絕
北京
1984 年 10 月 23 日

駐足門前見一斑，
難觀全豹悵徒然。
聲名早已揚天下，
宜佈真光育智賢！

163.　The Beijing University

In the Poetic Style of Qijue
Beijing
October 23, 1984

Making a momentary stay
In front of the gates,
I see a part,
Not the whole of the university,
As if seeing a spot,
Not the whole of a leopard.
This is a futile regret.
The university has won long ago
A renown in the world.
It should spread the light of truth
And rear the wise and the virtuous!

164. 遊天壇公園

七絕
北京
1984 年 10 月 24 日

淫逸驕奢或帝王，
蒼天知祭可褒揚。
兩壇風貌仍雄壯，
幾許遊人本未忘？

164.   A Visit To The Tiantan (The Temple Of Heaven) Park

In the Poetic Style of Qijue
Beijing
October 24, 1984

The emperors might have been wallowing
In power, arrogance, luxury, license and pleasures.
Yet,
They should be praised
For knowing to offer sacrifices to Heaven.
The appearances of the two mounds
Look still magnificent.
How many visitors
Have not forgotten their own origins?

165. 參觀人民大會堂

憶王孫
北京
1984 年 10 月 25 日

巍峨會堂氣沖天，
宏大輝煌極壯觀，
昭示人民作主焉！
枉民嘆，
早已黨之馬首瞻！

165.   Paying A Visit To The Great Hall Of The People

To the Tune of Yi Wang Sun
Beijing
October 25, 1984

The majestic hall shows a lofty spirit,
Being vast, splendid and grand.
It would like to proclaim
That the people are
The masters in the country!
With a futile sigh,
The people should follow
The lead of the Party
Long ago!

166. 凝望南堂

四言詩
北京
1984 年 10 月 26 日

慕名來訪，未見大名；
「愛國」招牌，玉立婷婷。

兩門緊閉，情景淒清；
今猶存在，慶幸堪稱！

定期開放，中外齊迎；
宗教自由，豈其證明？

166.   Gazing At The South Church

In the Poetic Style of Siyan Shi
Beijing
October 26, 1984

On account of your fame,
I come to visit you.
I do not see your formal name,
But a sign of the Patriotism,
Standing slim and graceful.

Your two gates are fast closed,
Leaving a scene, cold and deserted.
You are really lucky
To exist to this day!

Yor are open on certain fixed days
To welcome believers from home and abroad.
Can this be a proof
Of the religious freedom in the country?

167. 遊日壇公園

風蝶令
北京
1984 年 10 月 26 日

意善明清帝，
築壇祭太陽。
壇今成園眾觀光。
願世棄邪信主進天堂！

167.   A Tour Of The Ritan (The Temple Of The Sun) Park

To the Tune of Feng Die Ling
(The Butterflies in the Winds)
Beijing
October 26, 1984

With good will,
The emperors
Of the Ming and the Qing dynasties
Built the temple
To offer sacrifices to the sun.
Today,
The temple becomes a garden
For the people to visit.
I wish
The world will forsake evil
And believe in the Lord
To enter Paradise!

168. 參觀
中國革命歷史博物館

七絕
北京
1984 年 10 月 28 日

災難神州幾十年，
參觀史館悉由緣。
異端槍諜鬥批靠，
血淚史書中共編！

168.   A Visit To The Museum
Of Chinese Revolutionary History

In the Poetic Style of Qijue
Beijing
October 28, 1984

China, the Divine Land,
Has suffered catastrophes
For several decades.
By visiting this historical museum,
People may learn the reason.
Relying on the false and heterodoxy theories,
Guns, spies, struggle and criticism,
The Chinese Communists have arranged
The annals of blood and tears!

169. 入美簽證被拒

定風波
北京
1984 年 10 月 31 日

喜氣盈盈領館登，
何期掃興出門廳?!
負責官員當面拒。
何故？
去而不返意晶晶。

不有山窮河水盡，
忠薑，
怎逢柳暗又花明？
慈善萬能天父好，
緊靠，
定能飛往洛杉城！

169.   A Refusal To
My Entry Visa To The USA

To the Tune of Ding Feng Bo
(Calming Storm)
Beijing
October 31, 1984

I was happy to call at the consulate.
How did I expect
To leave the entrance hall in disappointment?!
The official in charge
Refused to my face.
Why?
My intention of not coming back after going in
Is very clear.

If where the mountains and streams
Do not come to an end,
For me, a faithful man,
How should I meet there
The shady willows and bright flowers.
But,
The loving-kind and Almighty Heavenly Father
Is good,
And depending on Him resolutely,
I am surely convinced that
I will be able to fly to the city of Los Angeles!

170. 人民英雄紀念碑

四言詩
北京
1984 年 11 月 4 日

天安廣場，碑聳入雲。
毛撰題詞，周寫碑文：
讚頌「英雄」，為共捨身；
「永垂不朽」，祝彼幽魂！
赤政屠心，奴役人民，
豈如斯碑，永世長存!?

170.   The Monument
To The People's Heroes

In the Poetic Style of Siyan Shi
Beijing
November 4, 1984

In the Tian'anmen Square
The monument towers to the skies.
The dedication by Mao Zedong
And the inscription by Zhou Enlai
Pay tribute to the "heroes"
Who had laid down their lives
For the Communist Party;
And wish "Eternal Glory"
To those ghosts!
The Red regime slaughters
The heart and the mind
And enslaves the people.
How could it remain
Like this monument,
Forever and forever!?

171. 遊碧雲寺

浣溪沙
北京
1984 年 11 月 8 日

羅漢漆金五百尊，
金剛寶座塔凌雲，
中山遺物殿中存。

堂殿六層林蔭裡，
鳴蟬泉水亦迎賓，
徐徐觀賞曠心神。

171.   A Tour To
The Temple Of Azure Clouds

To the Tune of Huan Xi Sha
(Yarn Wasked in the Stream)
Beijing
November 8, 1984

The gilded statues of the Arhats,
The disciples of Buddha,
Are five hundred.
The pagoda of the throne
Of Buddha's warrior attendants
Towers to the skies.
Something left behind from Sun Zhongshan
Were preserved in a hall.

The six halls tier upon tier
Are in the shadowy woods.
Singing cicadas and spring water
Greet also the guests,
Refreshing their minds and hearts
In slowly viewing and admiring.

172. 參觀
中國歷史博物館

七絕
北京
1984 年 11 月 10 日

中華歷史五千年，
文物古今實壯觀。
圖表解說多轉調，
神州老嫗變紅顏！

172.   Visiting
The Museums Of Chinese History

In the Poetic Style of Qijue
Beijing
November 10, 1984

Chinese history
Is as long as five thousand years.
The cultural and historical relics
Of the past and present
Are a magnificent sight.
The diagrams and illustrations
Sang a different tune!
The Divine Land has changed
From an old woman
To a beautiful lady!

173. 晨操

七絕
北京
1984 年 11 月 11 日

戶外晨操多處見，
老青婦幼欲身強。
欣欣景象堪稱道。
培育心靈亦莫忘！

173.   Morning Drills

In the Poetic Style of Qijue
Beijing
November 11, 1984

Outdoor morning exercises
Are seen in many places.
Old and young men,
Women and children,
All of them
Want to build their bodies.
This exuberant sight
May be praised.
They should also not forget
To cultivate their hearts and minds!

174. 觀覽地壇

卜算子
北京
1984 年 11 月 14 日

壯麗地龐然，
承載施恩典。
明代世宗建此壇，
敬謝犧牲獻。

大地實無知，
安作神明看？
啟示**真光**不照臨，
真偽誰能辨?!

174.   Seeing The Sight Of The Altar To The Earth

To the Tune of Pu Suan Zi
(The Fortune Teller)
Beijing
November 14, 1984

The earth is majestic, splendid and immense,
Bestowing upon human being
The favor of carrying them.
Shizong, the emperor of the Ming Dynasty,
Had this altar built
To offer to it sacrifices
In honor and thanksgiving.

The earth is really senseless.
How could it be regarded as a god?
If the revealed true Light
Does not illuminate,
Who will be able to distinguish
Between truth and falsehood?!

175. 入美簽證終獲

人月圓
北京
1984 年 11 月 15 日

早晨電話鈴聲響，
接聽暖心田。
立奔領館，
面談領事，
簽證恩頒。

傳音黃鐸，
電函修院，
散盡雲煙。
譯員領事，
齊聲祝願：
一路平安！

175.   Obtaining Finally My Entry Visa To The USA

To the Tune of Ren Yue Yuan
(The Family Reunion and the Full Moon)
Beijing
November 15, 1984

In the morning
A phone call rang me up;
I went to answer,
Feeling my heart warmed.
I hastened at once to the consulate.
After an interview with the consul,
I was graciously granted
The entry visa.

With transmitting the messages by Fr. Bernard,
With telephoning and writing by the monastery,
All the clouds and smokes
Have been scattered.
The interpreter and the consul
Wish me, in unison,
A pleasant journey!

176. 出境回執

生查子
北京
1984 年 11 月 17 日

昨天三部門，
馬不停蹄跑。
三吃閉門羹，
依舊無煩惱。

再奔今早晨，
堅毅收成效。
發證局公安，
謝主安排妙！

176.   The Exit Receipt

To the Tune of Sheng Zha Zi
(Fresh Berries)
Beijing
November 17, 1984

Yesterday,
Three departments
I, as a running horse,
Went about calling one after another,
Without a stop.
For three times
I found the doors slammed in my face;
Still,
I was not upset.

This morning,
I hastened there once more;
Perseverance yields results.
The Public Security Bureau
Issued to me the document.
I thank the Lord
For His wonderful arrangements!

177. 題照告別
郎毓秀教授和蕭濟醫生

七律
北京
1984 年 11 月 20 日

深恩厚誼永難忘，
惜別依依欲斷腸！
四度登門蒙接待，
數回奉牘逝迷茫。
聊呈小照申心意，
誓把餘生獻上蒼。
不怨世間難再晤，
卻望歡聚在天鄉！

177. Farewell Dedication On A Photograph To Professor Pansy Lang Yuxiu And Dr. Michel Xiao Ji

In the Poetic Style of Qilu
Beijing
November 20, 1984

Your profound kindness and friendship
Will never be forgotten.
In saying goodbye reluctantly.
I am heartbroken!
Four times while calling at your house,
I was received.
Several times while receiving your letters,
My haze vanished.
I present respectfully a photogroph of myself
To extend to you my regard and gratitude.
I swear to dedicate
All my remaining years to Heaven.
I will not complain of
The difficulty of our reunion on earth;
But,
I would like to wish
A joyous regathering in the Heavenly homeland!

178. 題照告別
鐵窗好友傅志雄

玉蝴蝶
北京
1984 年 11 月 22 日

英文膚淺肢殘，
求允勉為難。
共學一年歡，
離監惜我先。

頻繁通信札，
重晤卻無緣。
愚即美西遷，
祝君前景爛！

178.   Farewell Dedication On A Photograph To Mr. Fu Zhixiong, A Good Friend In Prison

To the Tune of Yu Hudie
(The Jade Butterfly)
Beijing
November 22, 1984

My English was meager,
And one of my limbs disabled.
I reluctantly accepted your request
For teaching,
A task, difficult and even beyond my power.
We rejoiced to study together for one year.
It was a pity
That I left the prison before you.

We corresponded frequently;
But we had no good fortune to meet again.
Presently,
I am about moving
To the American West.
I wish you a bright future!

179. 題照告別
昔日獄友辛大榮

四言詩
北京
1984 年 11 月 22 日

同囚蓬安，勞改數秋；
喜獲同情，恩記心頭。

出獄不久，偶遇果州；
互致問候，前程各謀。

獲親友助，今往美洲，
訣別在即，寄照念留！

179.   Farewell Dedication On A Photo To Mr. Xin Darong, A Former Fellow Prisoner

In the Poetic Style of Siyan Shi
Beijing
November 22, 1984

Imprisoned together in Peng'an,
We did the forced labor
For several autumns.
I was glad to obtain your compassion;
I have kept your kindness in my heart.

Not long after each released from prison,
We met by chance
In Nanchong, in the old Guo Zhou;
We exchanged greetings,
But each of us was seeking his own future.

Thanks to the help of my relatives and friends,
I am now going to the America.
Parting with you before long,
I mail to you this photo
As a souvenir!

180. 辭別北京

七絕
北京
1984 年 11 月 27 日

乘車清早往機場，
旭日送行萬道光。
平順過關艙位入，
京師告別謝穹蒼。

180.   Bidding Farewell To Beijing

In the Poetic Style of Qijue
Beijing
November 27, 1984

Early in the morning,
By riding in a bus,
I went to the airport.
The rising sun escorted me
With shining a myriad of rays.
Having passed throught smoothly the checkpoints
And taken my cabin seat,
I bid goodbye to the capital,
And I give my gratitude to Heaven!

181. 路過東京

七絕
日本東京
1984 年 11 月 27 日

首都聲譽未虛傳，
夜景輝煌展眼前。
島國人民彌奮進，
京城風貌愈斑斕。

181.   Passing Through Tokyo

In the Poetic Style of Qijue
Tokyo, Japan
November 27, 1984

The reputation of the capital
Is not a false account.
The brilliant night scene
Appears before our eyes.
When the people of the island country
Continue advancing bravely,
The appearance of their capital
Will surely be brighter.

182. 謝謝好旅伴：
琳達・克勒滿女士、
博伊德・哈彌爾頓先生
和肯尼思・尼爾先生

憶江南
洛杉磯
1984 年 11 月 27 日

三旅伴，
幾度慨來援。
座位相鄰萍水遇，
關懷照顧記心間。
賜福望蒼天！

182.   Thank You,
My Good Fellow Travelers:
Ms. Linda Cleman, Mr. Boyd Hamilton
And Mr. Kenneth Neil

To the Tune of Yi Jiang Nan
(Remembering the South of the River)
Los Angeles
November 27, 1984

You,
My three fellow travelers,
Came generously to my help
Several times.
Our seats were close to each other,
Our meeting by chance
Was just like patches of drifting duckweed.
Your care and concern
Are kept in my mind.
I hope
Heaven will give you His blessing!

183. 修院家園
勝利返

人月圓
聖安德肋修院
1984 年 11 月 27 日

秋高氣爽陽光燦，
勝利返家園。
狂瀾強阻，
重洋遠隔，
三十三年。

耶穌助戰，
鬥毆鐐銬，
敗陣連連。
挺胸離獄，
昂頭出境，
終慶團圓！

183.   Return To My Monastic Home In Triumph

To the Tune of Ren Yue Yuan
(The Family Reunion and the Full Moon)
St. Andrew's Priory
November 27, 1984

In high autumn and bracing weather,
In bright sunlight,
I return to my monastic home
In triumph.
I had been obstructed forcibly
By the raging waves,
And separated greatly
By the seas and oceans
For thirty-three years.

With Jesus assisting in fighting,
I had defeated again and again
The struggle meetings, beatings, shackles and handcuffs.
Throwing out my chest,
I departed from prison;
Holding my head high,
I left the country.
Now, finally,
I celebrate my reunion with my monastery!

184. 題照贈
神學生
阿伯托·魯易先生

六言詩
聖安德肋修院
1984 年 12 月 8 日

作客君住鄰室，
前晚應邀往訪。
遵囑題詞聖書，
蒙饋精緻苦像。

欣悉領品在即，
告以自身情況。
茲獻小照致謝，
錦繡前程祝望！

184.   Dedication On A Photo To A Seminarian, Mr. Alberto Ruiz

In the Poetic Style of Liuyan Shi
St. Andrew's Priory
December 8, 1984

You, a guest, stay in the neighboring room.
At your invitation,
I visited you at night before last.
At your request,
I wrote a few words
In your holy book.
I was given a delicate crucifix.

I was glad
To learn your forthcoming priestly ordination.
I told you my own situation.
Now,
In thanksgiving,
I present you a photo.
I wish you a splendid future!

185. 辭歲主前

七律
聖安德肋修院
1984 年 12 月 31 日

胸次波濤滾滾翻，
情懷憶往欲言宣。
重重關卡全衝破，
耿耿忠心奏凱旋。
艱苦鬥爭收績效，
香甜美夢盼能圓。
幸離鐵幕深恩謝。
經歷成書猶待援！

185.   Bidding Farewell
To The Outgoing Year
In The Presence OF The Lord

In the Poetic Style of Qilu
St. Andrew's Priory
December 31, 1984

Like raging waves surge in my heart,
My thoughts and feelings
For recalling the past
Want to be expressed in words.
Multiple checkpoints
Were all broken through successively;
A dedicated loyal heart
Won the battle.
My arduous struggle
Has achieved success;
My sweet dream
Is also expected to be realized.
Having fortunately departed
Behind the Iron Curtain,
I am grateful to You, O my Lord,
For this great favor.
To bring my experiences into a book,
I still wait for Your help!

186. 題照贈王淑玲小姐

搗練子
聖安德肋修院
1985 年 4 月 2 日

留學美，
志非凡。
彼此同胞喜晤談。
真諦人生望領悟，
未來前景祝斑斕！

186.   Dedication On A Photograph To Miss Wang Shuling

To the Tune of Dao Lian Zi
(Pounding Silk Floss)
St. Andrew's Priory
April 2, 1985

Coming to the United States to study,

You have an extraordinary aspiration.

Being fellow compatriots,

We rejoice to meet and talk

With one another.

I hope

You will realize

The true meaning of life.

I wish a gorgeous prospect

To your future!

187. 洛杉磯主教座堂
十一位執事晉鐸典禮

蝶戀花
洛杉磯
1985 年 6 月 15 日

十一青年蒙召選，
為舉樞機授品莊嚴典。
觀禮信徒堂內滿，
禱歌嘹喨沖霄漢。

主教座堂雄偉殿，
彩照窗中救主生平現。
主範遵從新鐸盼，
羊群牧放常勤勉！

187.   Priestly Ordination
To Eleven Deacons
In The Cathedral Of Los Angeles

To the Tune of Die Lian Hua
(Butterflies Courting Flowers)
Los Angeles
June 15, 1985

Eleven young men have been called and chosen.
The Cardinal holds a solemn priestly ordination
For them.
The Cathedral is crowded with attending faithful.
Prayers and chants soar to heaven
Loudly and clearly.

The Cathedral is a magnificent basilica;
The colored pictures on the windows
Show the life of our Redeemer.
We hope
The new priests will follow
The example of the Lord,
To tend their flocks
Always diligently and studiously!

188. 題照贈鄒逸蘭修女

蝶戀花
聖安德肋修院
1985 年 8 月 22 日

寶島出生紅禍免，
愛主情深、
慷慨童貞獻。
敝屣紅裝追聖善，
救人榮主懷宏願。

抗共多年忠未變，
靠主神通、
勝利桃園返。
異國相逢思赤縣，
同胞何日真光見？

188.　Dedication On A Photo To Sr. Theresa Zou Yilan, SSS

To the Tune of Die Lian Hua
(Buterflies Courting Flowers)
St. Andrew's Priory
August 22, 1985

Born in the Precious Island,
You avoided the Red disaster.
Your love for the Lord was so deep
As to devote generously your virginity to Him.
Having cast away colorful silk,
Like a pair of old shoes,
You pursued the holy and the good.
You cherished a great wish
Of saving man and glorifying the Lord.

In my many years' struggle against Communism,
My loyalty was unchanged.
Depending on the divine power of the Lord,
I came back victoriously
To this haven of peace.
In meeting with you
In this foreign land,
I think of China:
On what day will our fellow countrymen
See the light of truth?

189. 會晤鄉親
郭道芳女士

四言詩
聖安德肋修院
1985 年 9 月 28 日

風和日麗，**秋節**良辰，
化漠迎來，遊人友賓。

異域他鄉，喜晤鄉親；
巴蜀景物，記憶猶新。

長住**寶島**，行善施仁；
育人弘道，壯志凌雲。

代馬依風，**大陸**望頻；
國復**教**興，究在何春？

189.   A Meeting With Ms. Guo Daofang, A Fellow Countrywoman

In the Poetic Style of Siyan Shi
St. Andrew's Priory
September 28, 1985

With gentle breeze and bright sunshine,
The Fall Festival is a fine day.
Valyermo welcomes
Visitors, friends and guests.

In this foreign country and alien land,
I rejoice to meet you,
A fellow countrywoman.
This reminds my memory still fresh
Of the scene of our Chongqing and Sichuan.

Living in the Precious Island
For a long time,
You have done good deeds,
Performed benevolence,
Educated students and glorified the truth.
Your lofty aspitations soar to the skies.

Like a horse of the Hu,
The northern and western minority Chinese,
In the north wind,
I have looked back frequently
To the Mainland from long distance.
The restoration of the country
And the rejuvenation of the Church,
In what spring this will actually be?

190. 再訪
西雅圖貞女山堂

如夢令
華盛頓州西雅圖
1985 年 12 月 8 日

來到寒冬已久，
北國風光依舊。
訪問再今朝，
重晤鄉親良友。
良友，
良友，
無玷童貞常祐！

190.   Another Visit To
The Mountain Virgin Church
In Seattle

To the Tune of Ru Meng Ling
(Like a Dream)
Seattle, Washington
December 8, 1985

The cold winter has come
Already for a long time;
But the northern scenery
Remains the same.
Today,
In my second visit,
I see again
My fellow countrymen, my good friends.
My good friends,
My good friends,
May the Immaculate Virgin
Bless you always!

191. 同班韓國學友
桑・帕克太太
偕夫君、小孩
和妹妹來機場送行

定風波
俄勒岡州波特蘭
1985 年 12 月 14 日

一住俄城瞬七旬，
同班同級學英文。
嘗告自身曾獄陷。
銘感，
送行送禮竟今晨。

東亞山河長赤化，
牽掛，
何時祖國得翻身？
艙外太陽威又煦；
求主，
烏雲早逐救黎民！

191.   My Korean Classmate, Mrs. Sun Pak, With Her Husband, Little Child And Sister Comes To The Airport To See Me Off

To the Tune of Ding Feng Bo
(Calming Storm)
Portland, Oregon
December 14, 1985

I stayed in Oregon City
For seventy days, in a flash.
We studied English
In the same class and the same grade.
I have once told you
About my being put in prison.
I am very thankful to you
For your coming to see me off
And to bring me your gifts this morning.

The mountains and rivers in East Asia
Have been long Sovietized.
I am worried.
When will our motherlands
Be turned over and liberated?
The sun outside the cabin
Is powerful, warm and gentle;
I entreat the Lord,
In saving the people,
To drive out the dark clouds
As early as possible!

192. 告別俄勒岡市

定風波
俄勒岡市
1985 年 12 月 14 日

兩月居留秀麗城，
驪歌今唱道離情。
英語未能多進展，
何怨？
譯文自傳已成形。

二院二堂曾往訪，
舒暢，
友師學院意真誠。
新舊詩詞常賦譯，
胸臆，
與人分享喜盈盈！

192.   Bidding Farewell To
Oregon City

To the Tune of Ding Feng Bo
(Calming Storm)
Oregon City
December 14, 1985

For two months
I have stayed in the beautiful city.
Now I sing a farewell song to you
To express my parting feelings.
I did not make a little more progress
In learning English.
What is there to be grumbled about?
The translation of my autobiography
Has taken shape.

In the visits
To two monasteries and two parishes
I rejoiced.
The classmates and teachers in the college
Are sincere.
I have often composed and translated
My new and old poems.
Thus,
Sharing my sentiments with others,
I have felt happy!

193. 往訪
莫德‧杉布魯克教授

浪淘沙
聖安德肋修院
1986 年 2 月 1 日

故國在天邊，
鬼躪多年；
長期與戰凱旋歡。
主復施恩來美國，
與院團圓。

相識好機緣，
邀訪家園；
君鄉**海地**美江山。
文化**神州**聞講述，
樂也陶然！

193.   Visiting Professor Maud Shambrook

To the Tune of Lang Tao Sha
(Wave-Wasked Sands)
St. Andrew's Priory
February 1, 1986

My motherland
Is far away to the ends of the earth,
Trampled underfoot by monsters for many years.
Having fought against them
For a long, long time,
I was overjoyed to gain a victory.
The Lord bestowed on me also
The favor of coming to America
To rejoin my original monastery.

I was given a lucky chance
To be acquinted with you
And to be invited to visit your home.
Your native land, Haiti,
Has beautiful rivers and mountains.
Hearing you talking about the Chinese culture,
I am happy and rejoicing!

On May 17, 2001, in the afternoon, during his stay as a guest in Marie-Therese Thoreau's house in Ambourg, Belgium, Br. Peter(C) with Anne Deprez(L), a new friend, and his hostess (R), taken in her house.

2001年5月17日下午，在比利時昂布爾瑪利亞－德肋撒‧托洛家客居期間，筆者（中）和新友安娜‧德普雷（左）與女主人（右）合影於東道家。

On May 17, 2001, in the afternoon, Br. Peter (C) visits Anne Deprez's community in Liege, La Fraternite d'Eglise Liege-Chine.

2001年5月17日下午，筆者（中）參觀了安娜‧德普雷在列日的團體，「天主教列日－中國友愛會」。

On May 17, 2001, in the afternoon, Br. Peter (C) recites in their parlour to the members of Anne Deprez's community his French speech, translated by Frederique Barloy, about his experiences of resisting the Chinese Communist religious persecution.

2001年5月17日下午，筆者（中）在他們的客廳，向安娜‧德普雷團體的成員，朗誦了他的由費敏翻譯的關於他抵抗中共宗教迫害的經歷的法文講稿。

On May 20, 2001, Br. Peter (C) in front of the cave where Our Lady of Lourdes appeared, taken by Frederique Barloy, his financial helper and companion of this pilgrimage.

2001 年5月20日，筆者（中）立於露德聖母顯現的山洞前，由費敏拍攝，她是筆者這次朝聖之旅的資助者和旅伴。

On April 16, 2006, at 1:20 am, after the Easter Vigil, Br. Peter (second left) with his editor, Fr. Simon J. O'Donnell (second right), his close Korean friend and sponsor, Christina Kim (L) and her daughter, Amanda Kim (R) in the monastery refectory.

2006 年4月16日，在復活節前夕守夜禮後的一點二十分鐘，筆者（左二）與他的審稿者西滿‧奧多尼爾神父（右二）、他的贊助者韓國好友基督蒂娜‧金（左）和她的女兒阿曼達‧金（右），合影於修院餐廳。

On March 2, 2008, Sunday, Br. Peter's (C) close Korean friend, Christina Kim (R), visits the Abbey to celebrate the birthday of her daughter, Amanda (L).

2008年3月2日，星期天，筆者（中）的韓國好友基督蒂娜‧金（右），帶著女兒阿曼達（左）前來修院爲之賀生。

On April 6, 2008, in the afternoon, Jiang Guihua (C), the husband of Zhou Zhongzhen, Br. Peter's eldest niece, accompanies him to sightsee in the Shaocheng Park in Chengdu City, Sichuan, China.

2008年4月6日下午，筆者在中國四川的大姪女周仲珍的夫婿蔣貴華（中），陪同遊覽成都市少城公園。

On April 6, 2008, in the afternoon, Br. Peter's grandniece Jiang Yun accompanies him to sightsee in the Shaocheng Park in Chengdu City, Sichuan, China.

2008年4月6日下午，筆者在中國四川的姪外孫女蔣雲，陪同遊覽了成都市少城公園。

On April 6, 2008, in the afternoon, Br. Peter's eldest niece, Zhou Zhongzhen, accompanies him to sightsee in the Shaocheng Park in Chengdu City, Sichuan, China.

2008年4月6日下午，筆者在中國四川的大姪女周仲珍，陪同遊覽了成都市少城公園。

On April 6, 2008, in the afternoon, Br. Peter (C) with his grandnephew Jiang Jin, grandniece Liang Jie and their child Jiang Xuqi in the Shaocheng Park in Chengdu City, Sichuan, China.

筆者（中）與他的姪外孫蔣進、姪外孫媳梁潔和他們的小孩蔣旭麒，於2008年4月6日午后，合影於中國四川成都市少城公園。

Br. Peter with his second niece Zhou Zhongyu in Deyang City, Sichuan, China, on April 13, 2008.

2008年4月13日，筆者與他的二姪女周仲玉，合影於中國四川德陽市。

On April 13, 2008, Br. Peter (L) with his second nephew Liu Shiyin (R) in Deyang City, Sichuan, China.

2008年4月13日，筆者（左）與二姪女婿劉世銀（右）合影於中國四川德陽市。

On April 27, 2008, before taking a pleasure boat at the back in the river, Br. Peter on the bank of the Chang Jiang in Chongqing City.

2008年4月27日，筆者在搭乘背後的江中遊輪前，留影於重慶市長江岸邊。

On April 27, 2008, Br. Peter in front of the Chaotian Gate by the bank of the Chang Jiang in Chongqing City.

2008年4月27日，筆者留影於重慶市長江邊的朝天門前。

On May 4, 2008, Br. Peter in front of the former residence of Liu shaoqi in Huaminglou in Hunan Province.

2008年5月4日，筆者在湖南省花明樓劉少奇故居前留影。

On May 4, 2008, Br. Peter near the bronze statue of Mao Zedong in Shaoshan in Hunan Province.

2008年5月4日，筆者在湖南省韶山毛澤東銅像旁留影。

On May 4, 2008, in the morning, Br. Peter visits the former residence of Mao Zedong in Shaoshan in Hunan Province.

2008年5月4日上午，筆者參觀了湖南省韶山的毛澤東故居。

On May 23, 2008, Br. Peter climbs the sightseeing hall to the highest 88th story of the Jin Mao Mansion in Shanghai.

2008年5月23日，筆者登上了上海金茂大廈88最高層的觀光廳。

On May 23, 2008, in the afternoon, Br. Peter sightsees the Shanghai Beach.

2008年5月23日下午，筆者遊覽了上海外灘。

On May 24, 2009, in the evening dinner sponsored by the Visual Artists Guild in Los Angeles in California, Br. Peter (R) and Fr. Gerard O'Brien are on the platform given awards as Champion for Freedom of Religion.

2009年5月24日，在由加利福尼亞州洛杉磯「視覺藝術家協會」主辦的晚餐會上，筆者（右）和杰拉德・奧布賴恩神父上講台獲頒「宗教自由鬥士獎」。

On August 21, 2009, at the close of the burial of Fr. Eleutherius Winance in the Abbey cemetery, Br. Peter with Theresa Marie Moreau, his good friend and constant voluntary editor since August 2008.

2009年8月21日，在華倫士神父的葬禮將完時，筆者與好友和自2008年8月以來的經常的志願審稿人德肋撒・瑪利亞・莫洛女士合影於修院墓地。

On October 12, 2009, in Taiwan, under the guidance of Fr. Matthew Zhu Lide (L), Br. Peter (seated) visits the printer of his three books, the boss Jiang Baoqing (C) in the office of the Yeong Wang Cultural Enterprise Company in Taipei City, and Miss Yang (R), an employee doing the typing and layout of his books.

2009年10月12日，筆者（坐於前排）在台灣時，曾由朱立德神父（左）領往台北市永望文化事業有限公司辦公室，拜訪了承印筆者三本書的姜寶慶老闆（中）和負責打字編排的職工楊小姐（右）。

On October 19, 2009, James Mao Yongchang (R), Br. Peter's old classmate and then host in Taiwan, takes him to tour the Riyuetan (Sun and Moon Lake) in Nantou County.

2009年10月19日，筆者的老同學和當時旅居台灣的東道毛永昌（右），帶領遊覽了南投縣日月潭。

On October 19, 2009, Br. Peter's (L) host (R) takes him also to sightsee the Xuanzang Temple on the Guanghua Island in the Lake.

2009年10月19日，筆者（左）的東道主（右）還領他去參觀了潭中光華島上的玄奘寺。

On October 24, 2009, while staying in Taiwan, Br. Peter goes the second time to Dongshan Township in Yilan County to visit his fifth sister-in-law's family. (R-L): (front row) Br. Peter, his fifth sister-in-law, Wang Shuzhao; (back row) his eldest neptew's wife, Wang Lingyu and his eldest niece, Zhou Xiaozhen.

在2009年10月24日留台期間，筆者曾再次去宜蘭縣冬山鄉看望了五嫂家。（右起）：（前排）筆者、五嫂王淑昭、（後排）大姪媳王玲玉和大姪女周曉貞。

On October 24, 2009, in his fifth sister-in-low's house, Br. Peter (R) with his eldest niece, Zhou Xiaozheu (C), and his second niece, Zhou Zhonglan (L).

2009年10月24日，筆者（右）在五嫂家時與大姪女周曉貞（中）和二姪女周仲蘭（左）合影。

On October 24, 2009, Br. Peter with his fifth sister-in-law, Wang Shuzhao, in her house.

2009年10月24日，筆者與五嫂王淑昭在她家的合影。

470

A picture of the whole community of Br. Peter's (L) St. Andrew's Abbey on September 11,2010, taken at St. Mary's Church, Palmdale, California, after their new Abbot Fr. Damien Toilolo (C) having Received the Abbatial Blessing from the Most Reverend Gerald Wilkerson, Auxiliary Bishop of Los Angeles.

這是一張筆者（左一）的聖安德肋大修院全體修士 2010年9月11日的合照，拍攝於其新大院長戴米恩·托伊洛洛（中）在加利福尼亞州帕門德爾聖瑪利亞教堂，自洛杉磯至可敬的輔理主教杰拉爾·威爾克森領受大院長的祝福後。

Br. Peter (L) with his good friends and assistants to his workshop since 2010, Michaela Ludwick and her fiancé Maurice Russell; taken in the Abbey Bookshop on May 14, 2011.

筆者(左)與好友和自2010年以來的講座助手陸美珮和她的未婚夫莫里斯·拉塞爾，2011年5月14日合影於修院書店。

On October 2, 2011, Br. Peter with new good friends in the Abbey refectory: (R-L) Connie Guc, Br. Peter, Edna Tan and Genevieve Guc.

2011年10月2日，筆者與新好友合影於修院餐廳。（右起）倪美玲、筆者、埃德娜·譚和熱納維埃夫·卡克。

On October 2, 2011, Br. Peter with new good friend, Genevieve Guc in the Abbey refectory.

2011年10月2日，筆者與新好友熱納維埃夫‧卡克合影於修院餐廳。

On October 9, 2011, in the afternoon, Br. Peter (L) joyfully welcomes Ms. Annie Chen Yanjuan, a Chinese visitor, and her husband, son and friend on the Abbey grounds. He talks with her very happily and presents to her his three new editions.

2011年10月9日，筆者在修院場地喜迎中國客人陳燕娟女士、她的夫婿、兒子和朋友。筆者同她相談甚歡，並獻上自己的三本新版書。

On October 9, 2011. Br. Peter (L) with Mr. Louis Poreider (R), Ms. Annie Chen's husband, on the monastery grounds.

2011年10月9日，筆者（左）與陳女士的夫婿路易斯‧波里德爾先生合影於修院場地。

472

On October 9, 2011, Br. Peter (C) with Ms. Annie Chen's husband, Mr. Louis Poreider (L), and their son.

2011年10月9日，筆者（中）與陳女士的夫婿路易斯・波里德爾先生（左）和他們的兒子的合照。

On October 9, 2011, Br. Peter (L) with Ms. Annie Chen (second left), her friend, Ms. Lily He in the monastery small refectory.

2011年10月9日，筆者（左）與陳女士（左二）和她的朋友何女士，攝於修院小餐廳。

A picture of Br. Peter's good friends, Tom and Angie Miller, a married couple, taken on November 5, 2011, after Tom having been ordained to the Permanent Diaconate by His Excellency Bishop Rutilio Juan del Rivego.

筆者好友湯姆和吉安・米勒伉儷，於2011年11月5日，在湯姆由最可敬的魯蒂里奧・關・德爾・里埃戈主教任命爲終身執事後的合照。

On November 22, 2011, Br. Peter with his good Chinese friend, Miss Terry Qin Lijun, on the monastery grounds.

2011年11月22日，筆者與中國好友秦麗君小姐合影於修院場地。

On March 17, 2012, Br. Peter with his new friends, Angelo and Jenny Lamola, a married couple, in the monastery refectory.

2012年3月17日，筆者與新友安吉洛‧拉莫拉和李杰妮伉儷合影於修院餐廳。

On May 26, 2012, Br. Peter with his new friend, Ms. Jennifer Lee, on the Abbey grounds.

2012年5月26日，筆者與新友李賢洙女士合影於修院場地。

On October 31, 2012, Br. Peter with two employees of the Abbey on the monastery grounds: Br. Peter(c), Michael Kalina and his fiancée, Myla Malagubang.

2012年10月31日，筆者與本院兩位職工合影於修院場地：筆者（中），彌額爾‧凱利納和他的未婚妻邁拉‧瑪拉古邦。

On November 2, 2012, Br. Peter with five employees of the Abbey on the monastery grounds: (L-R) Rosalinda Nazario Pineda, Cheryl Evanson, Br. Peter, Sue Pressler (retired), Mary E. Kouf and Rita Jones.

2012年11月2日，筆者與本院五位職工合影於修院場地：（左起）羅莎琳達‧納匝里奧‧皮內達、徹麗‧伊文生、筆者、蘇‧普雷斯勒（已退休）、瑪利亞‧柯弗和麗達‧瓊斯。

On November 2, 2012, Br. Peter with four employees of the Abbey on the monastery grounds: (L-R) Rosalinda Nazario Pineda, John Lopez, Br. Peter, Mary E. Kouf and Rita Jones.

2012年11月2日，筆者與本院四位職工合影於修院場地：（左起）羅莎琳達‧納匝里奧‧皮內達、若望‧洛佩齊、筆者、瑪利亞‧柯弗和麗達‧瓊斯。

475

On November 5, 2012, Br. Peter with four employees of the Abbey on the monastery grounds: (L-R) Br. Peter, Lizzy Merritt, Neri Valladares, Randi Mailes and her husband, Ted Mailes.

2012年11月5日，筆者與本院四位員工合影於修院場地：（左起）筆者、莉齊‧麥里特、內里‧瓦拉達雷斯、蘭迪‧梅勒斯和她的丈夫特德‧梅勒斯。

On November 6, 2012, Maria Moore, an employee of Br. Peter's Abbey, in the monastery business office.

2012年11月6日，筆者本院的一位職工瑪利亞‧穆爾，攝影於修院庶務辦公室。

A family photo of Br. Peter's good friend, Karl Jennings, before Christmas in December 2012.

筆者好友卡爾‧詹寧斯的全家福，拍攝於2012年12月聖誕節前。

194. 參加基督蒂納・
金女士新居由本院大院長
方濟各・本篤主持的祝聖禮

七言詩
聖安德肋大修院
2003 年 7 月 26 日

初訪舊居七秋前，
彼此相識甫兩年。
茲登新居感觸深，
今昔情景異迴然。

主施考驗儘嚴酷，
亦賜力量勇承擔。
受傷蘆葦挺然立！
欲熄燈心繼續燃！

歲月流逝留痕跡，
東道友情彌拳拳。
祝願新居享寧靜，
天上家園且領還！

194.   Attending The Consecration Of Ms. Christina Kim's New Home By Our Fr. Abbot Francis Benedict

In the Poetic Style of Qiyan Shi
St. Andrew's Abbey
July 26, 2003

Seven autumns before,
I visited your former residence the first time;
We had then been acquainted just two years.
Now,
In calling at your new home,
I am deeply touched:
The present and previous sights are poles apart.

The Lord had once inflicted on you,
Though, a very grim trial,
He, yet, also lavished on you
The strengh to bear bravely.
The bruised reed could then stand upright!
The smoldering wick could continue burning!

The years and months have passed,
Leaving certain traces;
The friendship of the hostess is most sincere.
I wish your new home
Will enjoy peace and tranquility,
Even lead you to your Heavenly home!

195. 懷念
親密戰友呂金鰲

鷓鴣天
聖安德肋大修院
2006 年 11 月 9 日

朱鐸來鴻閱日中，
噩音霹靂震晴空；
教中戰士女中傑，
乘鶴西歸已兩冬！

真理衛，
校園中，
隻身四載搏**群熊**！
小街尊府常歡聚，
歷歷眼前音與容！

195.   Remembering Lu Jin'ao, An Intimate Battle Companion

To the Tune of Zhegu Tian
(The Sky of Partridges)
St. Andrew's Abbey
November 9, 2006

At midday
When reading the letter from Fr. Matthew Zhu Lide,
I was shaken by the sad news
As by a bolt from the blue:
You, Jin'ao,
Champion of the Church and heroine,
Riding the Crane,
Journeyed home to the West
Already two winters passed!

Defending the Truth
In the university,
You all alone fought a host of Bears
For four years!
We often happily gathered
In your home on the narrow street;
Your voice and countenance
Leap up still vividly before my eyes!

196. 再訪吉爾伯特 · 賈維茲執事先生和其妻多洛蕾 · 賈維茲太太

畫堂春
聖安德肋大修院
2008 年 2 月 24 日

時晴時雨近三天，
深情念載依然。
百人會上歷程談，
籌劃周全。

兩夜新居留宿，
再蒙關切支援。
効勞**教會**十三年，
執事欣歡！

196.   A Revisit To
Mr. Deacon Gilbert Chavez
And His Wife, Mrs. Dolores Chavez

To the Tune of Hua Tang Chun
(Spring in the Hall of Paintings)
St. Andrew's Abbey
February 24, 2008

During These three days,
Now it is clear, now it rains.
Your deep friendship remains the same
For twenty years.
At the gathering of one hundred people
I talk about my experiences.
Your arrangement has worked out very well.

I have stayed in your new home
For two nights.
Once more,
I have been blessed
With your care and support.
You have offered your service to the Church
For thirteen years.
You, my dear deacon, must be filled with joy!

197. 在太平洋上空

西江月
自洛杉磯飛往北京途中
2008 年 4 月 3 日

去國當年慶幸,
還鄉今日歡欣。
春花異域爽心身,
念又四年興奮。

橫渡汪洋大海,
燕京彼岸飛奔。
容顏故里望全新,
時代跟隨前進!

197.   In The Sky
Over The Pacific Ocean

To the Tune of Xi Jiang Yue
(Moon over the West River)
On the Way from Los Angeles to Beijing
April 3, 2008

In those days,
Leaving the country –
Felicitous and fortunate;
Now,
Returning the homeland –
Happy and joyful.
Spring flowers in the foreign land
Refresh my mind and my body,
Inspiring me during those twenty-four years.

Crossing the Pacific Ocean,
Our plane flies speedily
To Beijing, to the other shore.
My wishes:
My native place
Will have a totally new face,
Forging ahead with the times!

198. 抵北京機場

憶江南
北京
2008 年 4 月 4 日

長夜盡，
破曉抵燕京。
古老京都重晤喜。
恢弘亮麗候機廳，
旅客笑顏迎。

198.   Arrival
At Beijing Airport

To the Tune of Yi Jiang Nan
(Remembering the South of the River)
Beijing
April 4, 2008

Now,
When the endless night
Comes to the end,
When the day breaks,
Our plane arrives in Beijing.
I rejoice
In meeting the ancient and old capital
Once again;
The wide, bright and beautiful waiting hall
Welcomes travelers
With a smile.

199. 晤大姪女周仲珍、
她的丈夫蔣貴華
和他們全家
於成都雙流國際機場

憶王孫
四川成都
2008 年 4 月 4 日

機場出口晤親人，
熱烈氛圍殘體溫，
多載離愁散似雲。
正陽春，
鳥語花香緣草茵。

199.   Meeting My Eldest Niece, Zhou Zhongzhen, Her Husband, Jiang Guihua, And Their Whole Family At Chengdu-Shuangliu International Airport

To the Tune of Yi Wang Sun
(Thinking of Wang Sun)
Chengdu, Sichuan
April 4, 2008

At the airport exit,
I meet my relatives.
The loving atmosphere
Warms my crippled body,
And makes my anxiety
About my separation for many years
Vanish like clouds.
On the fine spring day,
Birds sing,
Flowers send forth fragrance,
And green grass looks like a carpet.

200. 成都懷舊

蝶戀花
成都
2008 年 4 月 7 日

二十四年離故里，
十有一春舊夢重溫喜。
寧夏老監何處徙？
樹中挺立於原地。

羊市街頭修院裡，
舊屋全由新式樓房替。
住戶定為蓉市委，
門前有哨無標誌。

200. Thinking Of The Past In Chengdu

To the Tune of Die Lian Hua
(Butterflies Courting Elowers)
Chengdu
April 7, 2008

After my departure from my hometown
Twenty-four yrars ago,
I am glad here
To revive my old dreams
Of eleven springs.
The bygone prison on Ningxia Street,
Where has it moved to?
The Shude Middle School
Still stands firm on its original location.

On Yangshi Street
In our monastery
Old houses have been utterly substituted
With new buildings of many stories.
The resident must be
The "Chengdu Municipal Committee
Of the Chinese Communist Party."
In front of the gates
There are guards,
But no sign.

201. 芙蓉城風貌新

虞美人
成都
2008 年 4 月 8 日

全新面貌芙蓉邑，
老馬途難識。
東奔西走累身心，
故地其他困憊懶追尋。

平安橋畔宏堂貌，
既變焉憑弔？
班房文聖或他移，
在否西門勞改廠紅旗？

201.   The City Of Hibiscus In A New Look

To the Tune of Yu Mei Ren
(The Beauty of Yu)
Chengdu
April 8, 2008

The City of Hibiscus
Has an utterly new look.
Though like an old horse,
I find it hard
To know the way.
To look for and to walk
This or that street,
I am so exhausted
In body and in heart,
Unwilling to search for
The other old places.

The face of the grand church
On Peace Bridge Street
Has been already changed,
Why could I possibly go to contemplate it?
The jail on Wensheng Street
Might have been moved to another place.
The Red Flag Ironworks, my labor-reform camp,
Is it still at the West Gate?

202. 作客
郎毓秀教授家

西江月
成都
2008 年 4 月 11 日

昔累登門求教，
今來拜謁請安。
精神矍鑠儘行難，
講課依然未斷。

來日去時盛宴，
熱情接待如前。
辭行謝意語難宣，
主祐安康惟願！

202.   A Guest At The Home
Of Professor Pansy Lang Yuxiu

To the Tune of Xi Jiang Yue
(Moon over the West River)
Chengdu
April 11, 2008

In the past,
Several times
I called on you for counsel;
At the present,
I have come to pay respects to you.
Despite difficulty in walking,
You are hale and hearty,
Still unceasing to deliver lectures.

On the day of my arrival,
And also at the time of my departure,
I am given a rich banquet.
Your reception is as warm as before.
At this moment of saying goodbye,
My gratitude to you is unspeakable.
But I wish:
The Lord will grant you
Blessings and the best of health!

203. 往德陽
訪二姪女家

漁家傲
四川德陽
2008 年 4 月 11 日

郎老朝辭車站去，
親人看望德陽赴。
一片綠秧和碧樹，
風裡舞；
田園景色多嬌嫵。

行李為提嘗兩度，
女郎旅伴溫良煦。
謝罷女郎出口處，
來姪女；
儀容喜見仍如故。

203.   Going To Deyang
To Visit My Second Niece's Family

To the Tune of Yu Jia Ao
(Fisherman's Pride)
Deyang, Sichuan
April 11, 2008

In the morning,
Having bid farewell to the revered Pansy Lang,
I went to the railway station
To leave for Deyang
To visit my relatives.
A stretch of green rice seedlings and virid trees
Dance in the breeze,
Showing a very charming rural scenery.

Having come twice
To help me with my baggage,
A young lady, my fellow traveler,
Is kind, good and warmhearted.
At the exit,
When I have just expressed
My gratitude to the lady,
My niece arrives.
I exult very much
In seeing that her appearance
Has remained the same as before.

204. 趕英趕美

漁家傲
德陽
2008 年 4 月 13 日

五十年前毛舌鼓，
紅旗三面神州舞。
總線躍進公社路，
全國步，
工農崩潰饑黎庶！

大廈德陽茲處處，
多車多廠多商鋪。
預告綠秧糧產富。
長勞苦，
「超英趕美」民方睹！

204. Surpassing The British And Catching Up With The Americans

To the Tune of Yu Jia Ao
(Fisherman's Pride)
Deyang
April 13, 2008

Fifty years before,
When Mao talked glibly,
The Three Red Banners
Danced in the Diving Land.
On the way of the General Line,
The Great Leap Forward
And the People's Communes
The whole country was forced to march forward.
Then,
The industry and the agriculture crumbled,
And the people suffered hunger!

Now,
In Deyang
There are tall buildings everywhere,
Also many vehicles, factories and markets;
The verdant rice seedlings in the fields
Herald a bumper crop of grain.
Having labored for a long, long time,
The people begin to see:
They are suprassing the British
And catching up with the Americans!

205. 惜別
姪女周仲玉
和姪女婿劉世銀

搗練子
德陽
2008 年 4 月 14 日

多載別，
喜重逢。
觀賞公園看市容。
來去匆匆如過客，
但望異日晤天宮！

205.   Reluctant Parting
With My Niece, Zhou Zhongyu,
And Her Husband, Liu Shiyin

To the Tune of Dao Lian Zi
(Pounding Silk Floss)
Deyang
April 14, 2008

After many years of separation,
I am elated
At seeing you again.
We go sightseeing
In the park and in the city.
As a transient traveler,
I hurry my coming and going.
But,
I hope
Some other day
We will meet each other
In the Heavenly palace!

206. 前注遂寧

憶王孫
四川遂寧
2008 年 4 月 19 日

仲珍作伴啟行程，
車抵遂寧陰轉晴。
故里新容美景迎。
鳥聲聆，
往事回思興奮情。

206.   Going To Suining

To the Tune of Yi Wang Sun
(Thinking of Wang Sun)
Suining, Sichuan
April 19, 2008

In the company of Zhou Zhongzhen,
I start on my journey.
When the sky changes
From gloomy to clear,
Our train arrives in Suining.
My native place welcomes me
With its new appearance
And beautiful scene.
Listening to the chatter of the birds,
I am excited
To recall the past.

207. 喜晤
嫂嫂王素貞、
三姪女周仲碧
和其夫宋華志

長相思
遂寧
2008 年 4 月 19 日

歲月長，
日月長，
別恨綿綿欲斷腸。
親人在遠方！

急還鄉，
見還鄉，
聚首交談樂滿腔。
蒙恩謝上蒼！

207.   Meeting Joyously
My Sister-In-Law, Mary Wang Suzhen,
My Third Niece, Zhou Zhongbi,
And Her Husband, Song Huazhi

To the Tune of Chang Xiang Si
(Enduring Love)
Suining
April 19, 2008

The years and months — long, long,
The days and months — long, long,
My parting grief,
Continuous and prolonged,
Has broken my heart.
My relatives are in a faraway place!

When I hurried to return to my native place,
When they see my coming home,
Then,
We are all filled with happiness
In gathering together,
In talking with each other.
For receiving this favor,
We give thanks to Heaven!

208. 遂寧：
旅遊名城

烏夜啼
遂寧
2008 年 4 月 21 日

廣靈古剎觀音，
匿山林，
古蹟輝煌、
遊覽客常臨。

涪江岸，
風光燦，
悅身心，
夜景靜觀、
踱坐撫提琴。

208.   Suining,
A Famous Tourist City

To the Tune of Wu Ye Ti
(Crows Cawing at Night)
Suining
April 21, 2008

The ancient Guangde Temple,
Lingquan Temple
And Guanyin, a Bodhisattva,
Are hidden in the mountain forests.
Tourists often come
To visit these splendid historic sites.

The bank of the Fu Jiang
With its magnificent scene
Pleases body and mind.
Pacing or sitting,
People watch the night view quietly
Or play the violin.

209. 漫步涪江邊

憶江南
遂寧
2008 年 4 月 22 日

如昔日，
漫步又江邊。
景物周遭全改變，
成真美夢已當年。
謝主滿心歡。

209.   Roaming Along The Fu Jiang Bank

To the Tune of Yi Jiang Nan
(Remembering the South of the River)
Suining
April 22, 2008

Like in former days,
I resume my rambling
Along the bank of the river.
The scenery around
Has completely changed;
My pipe dreams in those years
Have already come true.
Offering thanksgiving to the Lord,
I abound with joy.

210. 凝視
「四川省蓬安監獄」

浣溪沙
四川省蓬安錦屏鎮
2008 年 4 月 25 日

自果晨奔昔戰場，
春陽高照舊監牆。
新名門上放光芒。

苦戰十秋勞改隊，
裹屍馬革夢黃粱！
監傍慨嘆獻穹蒼！

210.   Gazing At The Peng'an Prison Of Sichuan Province

To the Tune of Huan Xi Sha
(Yarn Washed in the Stream)
Jinping, Peng'an, Sichuan
April 25, 2008

In early morning,
At dawn,
From Nanchong
I go to my former battlefield.
The spring sun shines from on high
Upon the old prison wall.
The new name on the gate
Radiates rays.

Here,
In this former labor-reform camp,
I fought bitterly
For ten autumns.
To die on the battleground
Was for me
Only a dream, an unreal dream,
Or a wish, an unrealizable wish!
By the jail
I offer my sigh and lamentation to Heaven!

211. 重睹修院
夕陽裡

清平樂
四川南充
2008 年 4 月 25 日

老家修院，
「天愛園」今變。
昔日院房全未換，
群像宗徒新建。

佘盧碑墓依然，
公墳苦路後山。
新貌聖堂展現，
舊觀恢復何年？

211.   Seeing Our Monastery Once Again In The Setting Sun

To the Tune of Qing Ping Yue
(The Qing Ping Song)
Nanchong, Sichuan
April 25, 2008

The monastery, my old home,
Has become "Heavenly Love Garden."
The old houses have not changed at all.
A host of Apostolic statues
Was newly constructed.

The tombs and monuments
Of Fr. Jehan Joliet and Fr. Gabriel Roux
Remain still.
The cemetery and Stations of the Cross
Are on the rear hillsides.
The chapel shows itself in a new face.
In what year
Will it be restored to its former look?

212. 注目
「四川省川中監獄」

浪淘沙
南充
2008 年 4 月 25 日

傍晚赴河東，
興致沖沖，
昔時省獄細尋蹤。
原址新名門上誌：
「監獄川中」。

囚此十一冬，
回味融融，
酷刑似火煉精忠。
奉獻精忠於上主，
榮幸無窮！

212.   Looking On Attentively
The Central Sichuan Province Prison

To the Tune of Lang Tao Sha
(Wave-Washed Sands)
Nanchong
April 25, 2008

At dusk,
I go to Hedong,
Bursting with enthusiasm.
I seek carefully
Traces of the old provincial jail.
At its original site
The new name on the gate is marked:
The "Central Sichuan Province Prison."

Over my eleven winters of imprisonment here
I ponder quite happily.
The cruel tortures as fire
Refined my loyal heart.
Offering my loyalty to the Lord,
I feel infinitely honored!

213. 告別南充

捣練子
南充
2008 年 4 月 26 日

相別後，
念餘春，
目擊容顏一片新。
蓮校座堂難訪恨，
省監修院見而欣。

213. **Leaving Nanchong**

To the Tune of Dao Lian Zi
(Pounding Silk Floss)
Nanchong
April 26, 2008

I have parted from you
More than twenty springs.
I see
Your face is all new.
Pitifully,
I fail to visit
The school by the Lotus Pond
And the cathedral.
But,
Gladly,
I see
The provincial prison
And the monastery.

214. 身在重慶

鷓鴣天
重慶
2008 年 4 月 27 日

車抵渝州未五更，
隻身初訪舊山城。
朝天門外訂船票，
明信片投郵政廳。

年老邁，
地疏生，
觀光名勝夢難成。
街頭徐步陪都憶，
肆虐日機焉炸平！

214.   I Am In Chongqing

To the Tune of Zhegu Tian
(Partridges in the Sky)
Chongqing
April 27, 2008

Before dawn
The train arrives in Chongqing.
All alone,
I come to this old hillside city
For the first visit.
I book a steamer ticket
By the Chaotian Gate;
I drop off my postcards
In the post office hall.

Senile,
Unfamiliar with the place,
I fail to realize
My dream of sightseeing scenic spots.
Walking slowly in the streets,
I remember this city in those years
Of being the secondary capital.
How could the Japanese planes,
Wreaking havoc, bomb it flat!

215. 魯熊・星城
庭園一日

漁家傲
重慶
2008 年 4 月 28 日

總部星城規劃妙，
高樓數十周圍繞，
還有池園亭閣島。
成效好，
洽談租售客常到。

無禁無詢無攪擾，
唸經靜坐深思考，
吟詠詩詞心境表。
斜日照，
起身謝主謝東道。

215.   One day In The Garden Of The Luneng Star City

To the Tune of Yu Jia Ao
(Fisherman's Pride)
Chongqing
April 28, 2008

Wonderfully designed,
The Main Office of the Star City
Is encircled
By decades of tall buildings,
And is attached
To a pool, a garden, pavilions and an island.
The effect is very good;
Customers come always to talk over
The business of rent or sale of the buildings.

Withour prohibition,
Without inquiries,
Without disturbances,
I come here freely
To say prayers and to sit quietly,
Pondering over deeply,
Or composing poems to express my mood.
When the sun is setting,
I get up,
Extending my gratitude
To the Lord and to the host.

216. 遊船過萬州

憶江南
重慶市萬州
2008 年 4 月 30 日

城遠望，
燦爛夕陽中。
林立高樓光彩放，
二橋江上似長虹，
時髦古都容。

216.   The Pleasure Boat Passed By Wanzhou

To the Tune of Yi Jiang Nan
(Remembering the South of the River)
Wanzhou, Chongqing
April 30, 2008

From afar
I see
The city glowing brilliantly
Under the setting sun.
Standing like trees in a forest,
Many tall buildings shine
With dazzling splendor.
The two bridges crossing the river
Look like rainbows.
The face of the city
Turns to modern from ancient.

217. 夜間過
長江三峽

憶王孫
湖北宜昌
2008 年 5 月 1 日

船過三峽夢猶甜，
隨夢飛逃好景觀。
兩岸猿聲早寂然。
艷陽天，
大壩雄姿入眼簾。

217.   Passing Through The Three Gorges Of The Chang Jiang At Night

To the Tune of Yi Wang Sun
(Thinking of Wang Sun)
Yichang, Hubei
May 1, 2008

When the boat
Passes through the Three Gorges,
My dream is still sweet.
With the dream
The magnificent landscape
Runs away swiftly.
From both banks of the river
The gibbons' howling
Has been silenced long ago.
On this bright spring day,
The majestic appearance of the Great Dam
Comes into view.

218. 別武漢

浣溪沙
湖北武漢
2008 年 5 月 2 日

賓館華坤哪裡藏？
火車車站匿何方？
東尋西問令神傷。

剛宿一宵今又別，
匆匆來去怎觀光？
火車頃刻過長江。

218.   **Departing Wuhan**

To the Tune of Huan Xi Sha
(Yarn Washed in the Stream)
Wuhan, Hubei
May 2, 2008

The Huakun Hotel,
Where does it hide?
The railway station,
Where does it conceal?
Looking for and asking about
Around here and there,
I am nerve-racked.

Just having stayed overnight,
I am now departing.
Coming and going in haste,
How can I do the sightseeing?
In a moment,
The train
Passes through the Chang Jiang.

219. 長沙

虞美人
湖南長沙
2008 年 5 月 3 日

深更半夜長沙到，
晨訂觀光票。
街傍靜坐享安閒，
往事舊情浮現在眉前。

火災抗戰初期歷，
早已無痕跡。
讀書革命十來冬，
毛自省城入主北京宮！

註：長沙大火發生於
1938 年 11 月 13 日。

219.   Changsha

To the Tune of Yu Mei Ren
(The Beauty of Yu)
Changsha, Hunan
May 3, 2008

In the depth of night,
I arrived at Changsha;
This morning
I booked a tour ticket.
By the street
I sit in quiet,
Peaceful and carfree.
Some past events, scenes and sights
Rise before my eyes.

In the early days
Of the War of Resistance Against Japan,
This city suffered a great fire,
Leaving no longer any vestiges of long ago.
For about ten winters,
Studying in schools and engaging in revolutions,
Mao started to go
From this provincial capital
Into Beijing, into its Palace,
And became the Master!

Note: The Changsha Great Fire took place
on November 13, 1938.

220. 天橋鬧市

生查子
長沙
2008 年 5 月 3 日

天橋夜景看，
目悅精神爽。
遠近萬千燈，
競把星光放。

乞憐四老殘，
美景無心賞。
枯坐傍橋欄，
苦臉行人望。

220.   The Overline Bridge In The Busy Streets

To the Tune of Sheng Zha Zi
(Fresh Berries)
Changsha
May 3, 2008

Watching the night scene
On the overline bridge:
A pleasure to the eyes,
A refreshment to the spirit.
Thousands of lights from far and near
Contest to radiate
Their rays, as starlights.

Begging for pity,
Four old, disabled people
Are in no mood
To enjoy the beautiful view.
They sit in boredom
Near the bridge railing,
Gazing on passers-by
With worried looks.

221. 紅太陽旅遊團

七律
長沙
2008 年 5 月 4 日

離開賓館天剛亮，
行李寄存車站傍。
西走東奔尋旅社，
左看右望結愁腸。
旅行社見談迷路，
女士容溫領廣場。
趕上遊車緣未失，
隨團觀賞好風光。

221.   **The Red Sun Tour Group**

In the Poetic Style of Qilu
Changsha
May 4, 2008

Just at daybreak,
Departing from the hotel,
I deposit my baggage
In the checkroom by the station.
I walk around here and there
To search for the travel agency;
I glance left and right,
Weighed down with anxiety.
Having seen the travel agency,
I tell them about my getting lost;
The lady is gentle and kind,
Taking me to the square.
I catch up with the tour bus,
Not losing the opportunity.
Now,
I join the group
To enjoy the wonderful sights.

222. 觀看
劉少奇故居

搗練子
長沙花明樓
2008 年 5 月 4 日

劉宅舊，
著新裝，
主席英名欲永芳！
十載含冤悽慘死！
斯居毛罪使彌彰！

222.   Viewing
The Former Residence
Of Liu Shaoqi

To the Tune of Dao Lian Zi
(Pounding Silk Floss)
Huaminglou Town, Changsha
May 4, 2008

Liu's original residence is old,
Now, newly dressed.
The Chairman of the state
May leave his illustrious name forever!
He suffered a wrong
For ten years,
Dying a miserable and tragic death!
This residence
May reveal a more obvious evidence
Of Mao's evil crimes!

223. 參觀
毛澤東故居

浣溪沙
湖南韶山
2008 年 5 月 4 日

一代梟雄**中共**神，
故居美化吸遊人。
豈能銅像義仁存？

家裡妻兒猶守候，
井岡逃往娶嬌珍。
棄珍後又與江婚！

註：毛的妻子是：楊開慧、賀子珍
　　和江青（李雲鶴、李進、藍蘋）。

223.   A Visit
To The Former Residence
Of Mao Zedong

To the Tune of Huan Xi Sha
(Yarn Washed in the Stream)
Shaoshan, Hunan
May 4, 2008

Mao was
A fierce and ambitious man of the age,
A god for the Chinese Communists.
His former residence has been beautified
To attract tourists.
How could justice and humanity
Exist on his copper statue?

While his wife and sons
Were still waiting home for him,
He took He Zizhen, a tender and lovely girl,
For his wife,
Soon after his escape to Jinggang Mountain.
Afterwards,
He discarded her
To marry Jiang Qing once again!

Note: Mao's wives: Yang Kaihui, He Zizhen
        and Jiang Qing (Li Yunhe, Li Jin, Lan Pin).

224. 深圳特區

漁家傲
廣東深圳
2008 年 5 月 6 日

三十春秋如水逝，
漁村化作大都市，
廣廈高樓隨處是。
特區史，
崎嶇燦爛宏而偉。

逃港饑民以萬計，
卅年前景浮胸際。
面對邊城新景氣，
思建議：
認清正道和真理！

224.   Shenzhen, A Special Region

To the Tune of Yu Jia Ao
(Fisherman's Pride)
Shenzhen, Guangdong
May 6, 2008

When thirty years pass away
As running water,
This fishing village
Has become a great city.
The city bristles
With tall and large buildings everywhere.
The history of this special economical region
Is rugged, splendid and magnificent.

Famine refugees,
By the tens of thousands,
Fled to Hong Kong.
That scene of forty years ago
Comes back to my mind.
Facing the new prosperity
Of the border city,
I offer suggestion:
Recognize the right way and the truth!

225. 廣州：羊城

憶王孫
廣東廣州
2008 年 5 月 7 日

羊城古邑著華裝，
容貌輝煌放彩光。
烈墓黃岡慕萬方。
寄殷望，
早獲自由石室堂！

註：黃花岡七十二烈士墓，
　　石室聖心大堂。

225.   Guangzhou, Yangcheng

To the Tune of Yi Wang Sun
(Thinking of Wang Sun)
Guangzhou, Guangdong
May 7, 2008

Yangcheng,
An ancient city,
Is gorgeously dressed,
Showing a splendid look,
Shining brilliantly.
The Mausoleum
Of 72 Martyrs at Huanghuagang
Is the admiration of all.
My high hopes:
The Shishi Catholic Church
Will gain its freedom very soon!

Note: The Shishi, Cathedral of the Sacred Heart.

226. 念六小時
火車上

浣溪沙
陝西西安
2008 年 5 月 8 日

駐足花城剛一天，
火車今坐赴西安，
行經五省路漫漫。

遙望華山心境爽，
城鄉沿路展新顏，
吟詩祈禱樂陶然。

註：廣州以其四季鮮花盛開，
　　享有「花城」之譽。

226.   Twenty-Six Hours On The Train

To the Tune of Huan Xi Sha
(Yarn Washed in the Stream)
Xi'an, Shaanxi
May 8, 2008

I stayed in Guangzhou,
In the City of Flowers,
Only one day.
Now I ride in a train to Xi'an.
I pass through five provinces;
The journey, the path, the road
Is very, very long.

Looking at Hua Shan from afar,
I am in a refreshed mood.
The cities and the countrysides
Along the way
Present to me a new look.
I feel happy and carefree
Composing poems,
Praying.

227. 看毛澤東窯洞

生查子
陝西延安
2008 年 5 月 9 日

行程經八時，
隧道念餘遇。
午後到延安，
毛洞黃昏睹。

驅珍迎美藍，
城滿風和雨。
日食一隻雞，
革命為緣故！

227.   Seeing The Cave Dwelling Of Mao Zedong

To the Tune of Sheng Zha Zi
(Fresh Berries)
Yan'an, Shaanxi
May 9, 2008

The journey lasts for eight hours;
I enconnter more than twenty tunnels.
In the afternoon,
I arrive in Yan'an.
At dusk,
I see Mao's cave dwelling.

Driving He Zizhen,
And welcoming the beautiful Lan Pin,
Mao created a scandal,
A scandal spread widely
And talked of all over the city.
He ate a chicken every day—
For the sake of the "Revolution!"

228. 人民幣上
毛頭像

浣溪沙
延安
2008 年 5 月 9 日

毛害人民數十冬，
徒孫徒子續盲從，
昭昭劣跡擲風中！

紙幣多年頭像印，
豈能頌德又歌功？
東風豈易壓西風？

228.   Mao's Head
On The People's Currency
(Renminbi)

To the Tune of Huan Xi Sha
(Yarn Washed in the Stream)
Yan'an
May 9, 2008

Mao did the people great harm
For several decades of winter.
His disciples and followers
Cntinued to follow him blindly,
Casting his obvious evil doings to the wind!

His head has been printed
On their paper currency
For many years.
How can this eulogize his virtues,
Sing his achievements
And let the East Wind
Prevail over the West Wind?

229. 假人民幣

菩薩蠻
延安
2008 年 5 月 9 日

工商經濟急增長，
市場紙幣流通廣。
真幣遍流行，
假鈔隨悄興。

假真先檢驗，
收幣諸商店。
現象似奇觀，
見而焉不嘆！

229.   **False People's Currency**

To the Tune of Pusa Man
(Strange Goddess)
Yan'an
May 9, 2008

As industrial and commercial economy
Increases rapidly,
The circulation of paper currency
Is also very big in the market.
Alongside the spreading of the true currency,
The false currency springs up
On the quiet.

Shops always examine the currency
Where true or not,
Before accepting it from the customer.
Seeing this phenomenon,
Seemingly as a marvelous spectacle,
I cannot help myself not to sigh!

230. 新月如鈎

清平樂
自陝西回四川途中
2008 年 5 月 10 日

離延昨晚，
今早西安返。
經久遍尋原旅店，
旋又急奔車站。

火車站似商場，
登車正照斜陽。
新月如鈎子夜，
崇山峻嶺穹蒼。

230.   The New Moon
Is Like A Hook

To the Tune of Qing Ping Yue
(The Qing Ping Song)
On the way from Shaanxi to Sichuan
May 10, 2008

Last evening
I left Yan'an,
This morning
I came back to Xi'an.
For a long time,
I sought the original inn all over;
Then,
I went to the railway station
In a hurry.

The railway station is like a market.
When we boarded the train,
The setting sun is shining.
At midnight,
The moon, the crescent, is
Like a hook;
There are high mountains in the sky.

231. 過廣元
憶王艮佐神父

蝶戀花
四川廣元
2008 年 5 月 11 日

五七年前遵共諭，
「三自革新」大纛高高舉。
狂狼猛衝天國土，
子民受害深而巨！

何在高官榮祿譽？
早已偕同貴體葬於墓！
獲救升天惟望汝！
北京歸化求天父！

231.   A Remembrance Of Fr. Matthew Wang Liangzuo While Passing Through Guangyuan

To the Tune of Die Lian Hua
(Butterflies Courting Flowers
Guangyuan, Sichuan
May 11, 2008

Filty-seven years ago,
In compliance with the Communist instructions,
You, Fr. Matthew, began to hold high
The big banner of the "Three Autonomies Reform."
The raging waves lashed violently
At the land of the Heavenly Kingdom;
The people of God
Suffered deeply and greatly!

Now, where were
Your status, honor, salary and reputation?
All had been buried
In the tomb long ago
Along with your noble body!
But, I wish
You will be saved and ascend to Heaven!
I pray also to our Heavenly Father
For the conversion of Beijing!

232. 再返溫江

采桑子
溫江
2008 年 5 月 11 日

出遊忽忽三週矣，
疲困心身。
興奮精神，
舊地重遊晤友親。

火車乘坐奔南北。
城市鄉村，
景色清新，
觀賞吟詩頌主仁。

232.   Coming Back To Wenjiang The Second Time

To the Tune of Cai Sang Zi
(Picking Mulberries)
Wenjiang
May 11, 2008

It is three weeks suddenly
Since I went on a sightseeing tour;
I feel tired out
In mind and body.
But my spirit is excited
By revisiting old familiar places
And meeting with my friends and relatives.

By train
I hastened my travel south and north.
In cities and countryside
The fresh and lovely scenery
I enjoyed very much,
And composed poems
To praise the Lord's mercy.

233. 汶川強烈地震

西江月
溫江
2008 年 5 月 12 日

午睡正酣床上，
樓搖屋動突然。
起隨姪女出房間，
鄰近公園避險。

儼若驚弓之鳥，
居民麇集公園。
園如軍隊野營盤，
還似特殊景點。

233.   A Strong Earthquake At Wenchuan

To the Tune of Xi Jiang Yue
(Moon over the West River)
Wenjiang
May 12, 2008

When I was napping soundly
In my bed,
Unexpectedly,
The building shook.
I got up
And followed my niece
To leave the house.
We went to the nearby park
To escape from the danger.

Just like birds startled
By the mere twang of a bowstring,
The neighboring residents gathered
In the park.
The park resembled
A field military campsite
Or a special scenic spot.

234. 夜宿火車站

西江月
成都
2008 年 5 月 16 日

汶震傷亡慘重，
救災全國緊張。
廣場車站似汪洋，
旅客湧如狂浪。

蜂擁遲延進站，
班車已去怏怏。
夜留車站大廳堂，
進入夢鄉休想！

234.   Overnighting
At The Railway Station

To the Tune of Xi Jiang Yue
(Moon over the West River)
Chengdu
May 16, 2008

The Wenchuan earthguake
Caused grievous causalities.
The whole country is intense
With relieving the disaster.
In the railway station square,
As in a vast ocean,
Passengers crowd as turbulent waves.

Because of the throngs,
Entering the station lately,
I am dispirited
To learn the regular train already left.
At night,
I stay in the station hall,
Not imagining
I may go off to dreamland!

235. 天有不測風雲

臨江仙
成都
2008 年 5 月 17 日

車票凌晨重購得，
疲勞纏繞心身。
長天不測有風雲：
居然車票失，
程未啟黃昏！

老漢來談車站外，
甜言信以為真。
騙遭票失豈無因？
理當天不怨，
責己莫尤人！

235.   **Unexpected Storm In Nature**

To the Tune of Lin Jiang Xian
(Immortal by the River)
Chengdu
May 17, 2008

Very early in the morning
I bought a railway ticket
Once again.
I am weary in heart and body.
A storm may arise
From a clear sky:
Unexpectedly,
I lost my ticket
And failed
To start on my journey at dusk!

A man came to talk with me
Outside the station;
I believed his sweet words
To be sincere.
I was swindled and lost my ticket.
Was there no reason for this?
I should not grumble against Providence,
But only blame myself, not that man!

236. 登上火車
去南京

憶王孫
成都
2008 年 5 月 18 日

大廳車站睡通宵，
半夜三更地震搖。
登上火車暮靄繚。
樂陶陶，
即到南京看大橋。

236.   Getting On The Train To Nanjing

To the Tune of Yi Wang Sun
(Thinking of Wang Sun)
Chengdu
May 18, 2008

In the station hall,
I slept the whole night.
At midnight,
An earthquake shook.
In the evening, cloudy and misty,
I got on the train.
Now,
I am happy and contended
About arriving soon in Nanjing
And seeing the great bridge.

237. 終抵南京

鵲橋仙
江蘇南京
2008 年 5 月 20 日

離蓉前晚，
抵寧今早，
兩夜難眠疲困。
碧空如洗送春光，
得沐浴、
心情振奮。

物資軍隊，
火車急運，
汶震災民濟賑。
客車繞道或徐行，
晚點到、
朝暉慰問。

237.   **Arriving In Nanjing, Finally**

To the Tune of Que Qiao Xian
(The Magpie Bridge)
Nanjing, Jiangsu
May 20, 2008

In the evning before last,
I left Chengdu;
This morning,
I arrived in Nanjing.
Sleepless for two nights,
I am tired.
Bathed in the spring rays,
Sent by the cloudless blue sky,
I feel excited in mind and heart.

Trains urgently transport
Needed goods, materials and troops
To relieve the people
Suffering from the Wenchuan earthquake.
Our passenger train
That moved often by a roundabout route
Or in slowness,
Arrived late,
But is now saluted by the morning sun.

238. 南京

臨江仙
南京
2008 年 5 月 20 日

綠水青山環四面，
猶存風韻六朝。
秦淮畫舫好嬌嬈。
古都身影秀，
風裡自飄搖。

時髦風吹三十載，
直衝氣概雲霄。
容光姿態麗今朝。
幽情思古發，
觸景喜眉梢。

238. Nanjing

To the Tune of Lin Jiang Xian
(Immortal by the River)
Nanjing
May 20, 2008

Surrounded by blue waters and green hills,
Nanjing still retains
Some charms of its old, six dynasties.
Gaily painted pleasure boats
In the Qinhuai He
Look enchantingly beautiful.
The silhouette of this ancient capital
Is pretty,
Swaying with the wind freely.

During the last thirty years,
When the fashionable wind blew,
The spirit of this city
Soared to the skies.
Today,
Its appearance and posture
Are fascinating.
Musing over things of the remote past,
Moved by the present view,
I am delighted.

239. 遊南京

漁家傲
南京
2008 年 5 月 20 日

車抵江寧剛進站，
旅遊立刻來開展。
橋上長江望四面。
隨往看，
朝天宮裡金鑾殿。

門寶中華牆內掩，
瞻園虎字神威顯，
孔像秦淮風韻燦。
天已晚，
中山陵墓難登覽。

239.   An Excursion At Nanjing

To the Tune of Yu Jia Ao
(Fisherman's Pride)
Nanjing
May 20, 2008

Upon the arrival of our train
At the Nanjing station,
My excursion started.
We stood on the Chang Jiang Bridge,
Looking all around.
Then,
We went to the Chaotian Palace
To see the emperor's throne room.

The treasure of the Zhonghua Gate
Was concealed in the wall.
The Chinese character Hu (Tiger) in the Zhan Garden
Showed its martial prowess.
The Statue of Kongzi and the Qinhuai He
Demonstrated their various splendid charms.
It was getting dark,
I failed to climb to sightsee
The Zhongshan Mausoleum itself.

240. 中山陵

七律
南京
2008 年 5 月 20 日

金陵俯瞰紫金山，
南麓陵園景壯觀。
力搗**清廷**功社稷，
誤容**赤黨**禍黎元。
故都黔首**皇軍**戮，
總統府門**紅幟**懸。
逝矣東流秋六十，
自由重獲在何年？

240.   The Sun Zhongshan Mausoleum

In the Poetic Style of Qilu
Nanjing
May 20, 2008

The Zjiin Mountain looks down at Nanjing;
The Mausoleum at the southern foot —
A magnificent view.
In exerting himself
To overthrow the Qing Dynasty,
Mr. Sun Zhongshan
Made contributions to the country;
In allowing wrongly with the Red Party,
He brought calamities to the people.
The common people of this former capital
Were killed by the Japanese Imperial Army;
Over the Presidential Palace's gate
The Red flag hangs.
Like the running water eastward,
The last sixty autumns have passed away.
In which year will liberty be regained?

241. 蘇州一日遊

蝶戀花
江蘇蘇州
2008 年 5 月 21 日

車抵姑蘇晨十點，
旅社人員名勝領遊覽。
徐達瞻園名將緬，
虎池藏有吳王劍。

往訪寒山非夜半，
風采運河船上曾觀看。
北塔八層登勇悍，
蘇州眼底欣然見。

241.   One Day Sihgtseeing
In Suzhou

To the Tune of Die Lian Hua
(Butterflies Courting Flowers)
Suzhou, Jiangsu
May 21, 2008

In The morning at ten,
The train arrived at Gusu (Suzhou).
The staff of the travel agency
Came to lead us to sightsee scenic spots.
The Zhanyuan of Xuda
Cherished the memory of this famous general.
In the little pond of Huqiu (Tiger Hill)
The sword of King Wu was hidden.

Our visit to the Hanshan Temple
Was not at midnight.
On the boat
We saw
The graceful bearing of the Grand Canal.
Climbing courageously
The last eighth story of Beita (the North Pagoda),
I delighted in watching
The city of Suzhou unfolding before my eyes.

242. 一日杭州

漁家傲
浙江杭州
2008 年 5 月 22 日

迷路遲歸車去矣，
下車進食徒然悔！
幸主召賢危困濟。
為聯繫，
原車送往新車至。

船上西湖觀景緻，
岳王廟述忠臣史，
映月雷峰神怪異。
靈隱寺，
燒香頂禮多居士。

242.   One Day In Hangzhou

To the Tune of Yu Jia Ao
(Fisherman's Pride)
Hangzhou, Zhejiang
May 22, 2008

Losing my way,
I came back so late
The bus had already left.
It was in vain
To regret
Stepping off the bus to take food!
Fortunately,
The Lord called a good man,
To help me in a desperate situation.
He used his cellphone
To get in touch with the travel agency.
Then, another bus soon arrived
To take me to rejoin the original bus.

From a boat
I saw the scene of the West Lake.
Prince Yue's Temple
Narrated the history of a loyal official.
The Yingyue Tower and Leifeng Tower
Were both imagic and mystical.
In the Lingyin Temple.
There were lay Buddhists
Burning joss sticks,
Paying homage to the idols.

243. 夜抵上海

搗練子
上海
2008 年 5 月 22 日

高速路，
快車衝，
頃別杭州入夜空。
僅歷三時申即到，
輝煌夜景似長虹。

243. Arrival In Shanghai At Night

To the Tune of Dao Lian Zi
(Pounding Silk Floss)
Shanghai
May 22, 2008

Along the freeway,
Our speedy bus,
Parting soon from Hangzhou,
Ran into the evening sky.
Only three hours later,
It arrived in Shanghai,
Meeting the night scene,
As brilliant as the rainbow.

244. 上海遊點滴

卜算子
上海
2008 年 5 月 23 日

金茂最高樓，
頃刻乘梯上。
隧道浦江兩岸連，
風韻車中賞。

遊客外灘盈，
滾滾江流壯。
古廟城隍香火飄，
人拜城隍像。

244.   A Bit of Shanghai Sightseeing

To the Tune of Pu Suan Zi
(The Fortune Teller)
Shanghai
May 23, 2008

The highest story of the Jin Mao Mansion,
We climbed up
By the elevator in a moment.
The graceful channel of the Huangpu Jiang,
Joining the two banks,
We enjoyed in the small train.

The Beach was crowded with exursionists;
The current of the river
Surged forward magnificently.
In the ancient temple of the town's guardian god
Joss sticks and burning candles fluttered;
People worshiped the statue of the guardian god.

245. 懷念佘山聖母

蝶戀花
上海
2008 年 5 月 23 日

一日留申真太短，
聖地佘山朝覲難償願。
身在外灘心在殿，
追懷聖母諸恩典。

往事舊情眉睫現；
五十年前聖像加金冕。
大陸孩兒長受難，
支援拯救慈親盼！

245.   Thinking Of Our Lady Of Sheshan

To the Tune of Die Lian Hua
(Butterflies Courting Flowers)
Shanghai
May 23, 2008

One day in Shanghai was really too short;
I failed to fulfill my wish
Of making a pilgrimage
To the sacred shrine of Sheshan.
Now,
My body is at the beach,
But my spirit, at the Basilica,
Recalling all the blessings
From the Holy Mother.

The bygone scenes and feelings
Rise before my eyes:
Fifty years ago,
The holy Statue was coronated
With a golden crown.
Your children on the Mainland
Have suffered for a long, long time.
We hope you, our Mother of mercy,
Will support and rescue them!

246. 重遊
王府井街

七絕
北京
2008 年 5 月 24 日

艷陽春日喜重臨，
店內新華書籍尋。
如織行人服飾麗，
吟詩觀景坐街心。

246. Revisiting Wangfujing Street

In the Poetic Style of Qijue
Beijing
May 24, 2008

On a sunny and bright spring day,
I delight
In coming to the street once more.
In the Xinhua Bookstore
I explore books.
People in beautiful clothes
Crowd as weaving.
Sitting on the bench
At the street center,
I watch the scene
And compose poems.

247. 再遊長城

憶王孫
北京
2008 年 5 月 25 日

滑車送我上名牆，
山嶺蜿蜒氣勢昂。
萬里**長城**萬里長。
照春陽，
欣賞再回好景光。

247.   A Revisit To
The Great Wall

To the Tune of Yi Wang Sun
(Thinking of Wang Sun)
Beijing
May 25, 2008

The pulley brings me
To the well-known Wall.
The Wall winds with the mountain ridges
Imposingly and majesticly.
The Great Wall is 10,000 lis (6,700km.) long.
Under the spring sun shining,
I enjoy once again the wonderful sight.

248. 自京回蓉火車上

漁家傲
四川成都
2008 年 5 月 28 日

兩夜一天車上寓，
唸經休憩詩詞賦。
車票幸而為臥鋪；
深謝主，
能眠夜晚和中午。

昨晚汶川餘震遇，
火車搖晃立停住。
經歷一時查線路；
無事故，
有驚無險平安度！

248.   On The Train
From Beijing Back To Chengdu

To the Tune of Yu Jia Ao
(Fisherman's Pride)
Chengdu, Sichuan
May 28, 2008

For two nights and one day
I stay on the train,
Reciting prayers,
Taking rest
And composing poems.
Because of my ticket for sleeping berth,
With deep gratitude to the Lord,
I can sleep at night and midday.

Yesterday evening,
The train runs into
An aftershock of the Wenchuan Earthquake.
The train rocks and promptly stops.
After an hour to inspect the line,
No accident is discovered.
We are alarmed,
Not in danger,
But in safety!

249. 女醫生：好旅伴

烏夜啼
成都火車站
2008 年 5 月 28 日

晨呼旅伴鄰床，
夢猶香：
「即抵蓉城速醒整行裝！」

提行李，
催車子，
示柔腸。
告別郎中酬報望穹蒼！

249.   A Woman Doctor, A Good Traveling Companion

To the Tune of Wu Ye Ti
(Crows Cawing at Night)
Chengdu Railway Station
May 28, 2008

Very early in the morning,
When my traveling companion called me
From the neighboring bed,
I was still in a sweet dream:
"Now, the train will be arriving
In Chengdu very soon.
Be awake quickly
To get your things ready!"

Having carried my baggage
And hired a taxi for me,
She was very Kind-hearted.
Bidding farewell to the docor,
I wished
Heaven would reward her on my behalf!

250. 三返溫江

如夢令
溫江
2008 年 5 月 28 日

歸返天猶未亮，
靜坐街邊默想。
破曉按門鈴，
重晤親人歡暢。
歡暢，
歡暢，
實現黃梁夢想！

250.   Return To Wenjiang The Third Time

To the Tune of Ru Meng Ling
(Like a Dream)
Wenjiang
May 28, 2008

Upon my return,
The day has not yet broken,
I sit on the sidewalk of the street
In quiet and meditation.
At dawn,
I ring the doorbell;
I am much elated
To see anew my relatives.
Much elated,
Much elated,
My fond dream is fulfilled!

251. 《明慧週報》閱後

如夢令
溫江
2008 年 5 月 31 日

《週報》偶看驚訝，
未潰「法輪」遭打。
弟子賀新年，
自美法師函謝。
華夏，
華夏，
旋里「自由」何夏？

251.   After Reading
The *Minghui Weekly*

To the Tune of Ru Meng Ling
(Like a Dream)
Wenjiang
May 31, 2008

Having read the "Weekly" by chance,
I am astonished:
Though oppressed,
The "Falun" has not been smashed.
To the New-Year greetings of his disciples
The master sent a letter of thanks
From the United States of America.
Oh, China,
Oh, China,
In what summer
Will your Freedom return home?

252. 暮晤姪外孫劉明

憶王孫
溫江
2008 年 5 月 31 日

由蓉來晤已黃昏，
往事童年猶憶新。
美好前程望勇奔！
正青春，
護佑懇求天地君！

252.   An Evening Meeting With My Grandnephew, Liu Ming

To the Tune of Yi Wang Sun
(Thinking of Wang Sun)
Wenjiang
May 31, 2008

At dusk,
From Chengdu
You came to see me.
The past of your boyhood
Is still fresh in my memory.
I hope
You will bravely pursue
Your glorious future!
Upon you, right now in your youth,
I entreat the King of Heaven and Earth
To bestow protection and blessings!

253. 郎毓秀教授禮品

西江月
溫江
2008 年 6 月 1 日

往謁慇懃接待，
今來親贈綢衣。
銀衫件件閃光輝，
修院人人蒙饋。

天各一方何礙？
友情萬縷千絲。
際茲告別感恩時，
長壽身安希冀！

253.　Gifts From Professor Pansy Lang Yuxiu

To the Tune of Xi Jiang Yue
(Moon over the Wset River)
Wenjiang
June 1, 2008

During my visit
You gave me an attentive reception.
Now,
You come here
To present us in person silk clothing.
Each silver shirt gleams.
Everyone in the monastery is offered one
As a gift.

Geographically,
We are far apart from each other,
But what does it matter?
Our friendship has been chained
So close as with countless links.
At this moment,
Saying goodbye and extending tnanks,
I wish you,
My dear and venerable Professor,
Good health and a long life!

254. 汶川大地震
二十天後

鷓鴣天
溫江
2008 年 6 月 2 日

卅萬傷亡竟造成，
且嘗汶震撼申京。
九千餘震還隨至，
慘景災情不斷增。

災賑款，
弊叢生，
稀疏雨點大雷聲。
全無預報何緣故？
誰是人民大救星？

254.   Twenty Days
After The Big Wenchuan Earthquake

To the Tune of Zhegu Tian
(Partridges in the Sky)
Wenjiang
June 2, 2008

Having caused injuries and deaths to 400,000 people,
The Wenchuan Earthquake
Shook also Shanghai, Beijing....
9,000 aftershocks followed;
New tragic scenes and disasters
Increased unceasingly.

The relief fund,
Because of many malpractices,
Was as if loud thunder,
But small raindrops
For the stricken people and areas.
Why no earthquake prediction?
Who should be
The great savior for the people?

255. 辭別大姪女周仲珍、 大姪女婿蔣貴華 和他們全家

漁家傲
溫江
2008 年 6 月 3 日

厚意深恩銘肺腑：
蒙邀探望川資付，
生活旅遊全照顧。
多鼓舞，
名都故地親身睹！

臨別惜難忠告吐：
崇高信仰須維護，
教誨公公牢記住。
齊敬主，
來朝天國恆歡聚！

255.   Bidding Farewell To My Eldest Niece, Zhou Zhongzhen, My Eldest Nephew, Jiang Guihua And Their Entire Family

To the Tune of Yu Jia Ao
(Fisherman's Pride)
Wenjiang
June 3, 2008

Your deep kindness and favors
Are engraved on my mind:
You invited me to visit you,
You paid the traveling expenses for me,
You took good care of my life and tours.
How was I inspired
To see famous cities and old places
With my own eyes!

At this parting moment,
It is pitifully hard
To pour out my sincere advice:
You must uphold your lofty Faith,
And you should keep firmly in mind
The instructions of your grandfather.
Let us venerate the Lord together
So that we may someday have a happy reunion
In the Kingdom of Heaven forever and ever!

256. 翩翩女士
好旅伴

漁家傲
北京機場
2008 年 6 月 3 日

行李助提來旅伴，
下機領往航空站。
手續轉機全為辦。
真友善，
攜包陪赴檢查站。

探望孩兒如所願，
北京工作今歸返。
有幸同機蒙照看。
謝款款，
主前默禱為芳範！

256.   An Elegant Lady, My Good Fellow Traveler

To the Tune of Yu Jia Ao
(Fisherman's Pride)
Beijing Airport
June 3, 2008

You, Oh, lady,
My fellow traveler,
Help me with carrying my baggage.
Getting off the plane,
You lead me to the station.
On my behalf,
You go through all the formalities
Of changing to another plane.
Really friendly,
Holding my handbag,
You accompany me also to the checkpoint.

Having visited your son
As you had wished,
Today,
You return to Beijing to go to work.
I have the good fortune
Of taking the same plane
And of being shown your concern.
Deeply grateful,
Before the Lord,
I pray in silence
For you, an excellent example of charity!

257. 美好歸國行

西江月
美國聖安德肋大修院
2008 年 6 月 3 日

兩月行程六萬，
尋遊故地原圄。
東奔西走不蹄停，
訪友探親覽勝。

慶未暈車生病，
風光悅目鄉城。
吟詩頌主訴衷情。
靜夜安還欣幸！

257. A Happy Trip Back To My Native Land

To the Tune of Xi Jiang Yue
(Moon over the West River)
St. Andrew's Abbey, USA
June 3, 2008

During two months,
I traveled 60,000 lis (30,000 km).
I located and toured
My old haunts and jails.
Rushing my journey east and west
Without a stop,
I visited
My friends, my relatives and some scenic resorts.

I rejoiced
To have never fallen carsick or ill.
The sight of cities and countrysides
Was pleasing to my eyes.
I composed poems,
Sang the praises of the Lord,
And poured out my heart.
In the quiet of the night,
I came back in safety,
With rejoicing and gladness!

258. 悼白澂明神父

鷓鴣天
聖安德肋大修院
2008 年 9 月 30 日

跌倒中風一月前，
回天乏術別塵寰，
多張粉畫飄雲彩，
祝願乘雲進九天！

迎大駕，
昔中原。
院房蓉建謝深焉。
什邡冬雪青城景，
粉畫精描且廣傳。

258.   Grieving The Death Of
Fr. Werner Papeians De Morchoven

To the Tune of Zhegu Tian
(Partridges in the Sky)
St. Andrew's Abbey
September 30, 2008

One month ago,
You, Fr. Werner, fell and suffered apoplexy.
Then,
When you reached the point of impossible recovery,
You left this world.
In many of your pastels
There are floating clouds;
I wish that
You are riding on those clouds
Into the Ninth Heaven!

One former day
We welcomed you to China.
We greatly appreciated your efforts
In the construction of the monastic building
In Chengdu.
The winter snow in Shifang
And the scenery in Qingcheng
Were delicately depicted in your pastels
And widely distributed.

259. 輓華倫士神父

西江月
聖安德肋大修院
2009 年 8 月 15 日

七十三年相識，
叨光受教多春。
「革新」堅抗志凌雲，
遭逐有榮無恨！

講道教書熱切，
暮年行視含辛。
依然百歲好精神。
今祝**天堂**欣進！

259.   Lamenting The Death Of Fr. Eleutherius Winance

To the Tune of Xi Jiang Yue
(Moon over the West River)
St. Andrew's Abbey
August 15, 2009

For seventy-three years
We were acquainted with each other.
I received your instruction and guidance
Over a long period of time.
In former days,
In China,
I followed you several times
When you visited Christian families.

You were very fervent
In preaching and in teaching;
You endured hardships
In walking and in seeing things.
A venerable elder of one hundred,
You remained still vigorous.
Now, we wish you
To enter Heaven with joy!

260. 飛往台灣

踏莎行
洛杉磯
2009 年 10 月 6 日

好友支援，
主施恩典，
三書正出新增版。
成真美夢訪台灣，
機場來到心歡忭！

易逝年華，
皺紋滿面，
夕陽光彩依然燦。
機艙靜坐湧歡波，
起飛銀燕沖霄漢！

260.   **Flying To Taiwan**

To the Tune of Ta Suo Xing
(Walking across the Meadow)
Los Angeles
Octber 6, 2009

With the help of my good friends,
With the kindness from the Lord,
At the time of the publication
Of the newly Updated editions
Of my three books,
To bring to life my beautiful dream
Of Visiting Taiwan,
I am cheerful and joyous
To arrive at the airport!

My years pass quickly,
My face is full of wrinkles.
The setting sun glow
Still looks brilliant.
When I sit in the cabin silently,
Feeling a wave of joy
Surging within me,
Our silver swallow starts its flight,
Soaring to the firmament!

261. 抵達
桃園國際機場

烏夜啼
台灣桃園
2009 年 10 月 6 日

飛臨寶島機場，
喜洋洋。
宏願多年、
今夜得終償！

東道急，
女兒覓，
晤門廊。
久別重逢、
共頌主慈祥！

261.   Arrival At
Taoyuan International Airport

To the Tune of Wu Ye Ti
(Crows Cawing at Night)
Taoyuan, Taiwan
October 6, 2009

Having flown to the airport
Of the Precious Island,
I am filled with great joy.
My great wish,
Cherished for many years,
Is finally realized tonight!

In the worrying of my host,
In the searching for of his daughter,
We meet each other at the porch.
Reuniting after a long separation,
We rejoice,
Singing together
Praises of the Lord's kindness!

262. 作客
老同學毛永昌先生家

生查子
台灣中壢市
2009 年 10 月 7 日

院離鄉井還，
另闢人生道。
入伍慶來台，
退役安居臺。

同窗曾六春，
來訪迎東道。
敘舊撫今朝，
謝主同歡笑！

262.   Staying As A Guest In The Home Of My Old Classmate, Mr. James Mao Yongchang

To the Tune of Sheng Zha Zi
(Fresh Berries)
Zhongli City, Taiwan
October 7, 2009

Leaving the monastery,
You returned to your hometown.
Then you began
To set up a new way of life.
Having enlisted in the army,
You were fortunate
To be able to come to Taiwan.
Today,
As an aged retired officer,
You live in peace.

We studied in the same class
For six springs.
Now,
Coming to visit,
I receive a welcome
From you, my dear host.
In talking about the past
And contemplating about the present,
We are grateful to the Lord in unison
With joy and laughter!

263. 收台北市
永望文化事業有限公司
三箱新書

清平樂
台灣中壢市
2009 年 10 月 9 日

時光流水，
半載匆匆逝。
伏案風霜天外置，
新版三書見喜！

抗魔衛教卅年，
跡留字裡行間。
主愛宣揚期望，
如泉滋潤心田！

263.   Receiving Three Boxes Of My New Books From Yeong Wang Cultural Enterprise Company Ltd. In Taipei City

To the Tune of Qing Ping Yue
(The Qing Ping Song)
Zhongli City, Taiwan
October 9, 2009

Time rushes by
Like running water;
Half a year passes away quickly.
Giving no thought
To the wind and frost
From the sadentary work,
I am joyful
In gazing at the three new editions!

I have campaigned against the devil
In defense of the Church
For thirty years.
The traces are left behind,
Between the lines.
I hope
They will publicize the love of the Lord,
And, as spring water,
Will nourish man's heart!

264. 喜晤朱立德神父

眼兒媚
台灣彰化
2009 年 10 月 10 日

驚濤**黃浦**襲**漁船**，
學子戰狂瀾。
坐牢卅載，
仍堅鬥志，
赴美終歡。

遷台勤學膺神品，
教難史修編。
出書念冊，
福民利國。
興**教**榮天！

264.   Rejoicing To Meet With Fr. Matthew Zhu Lide

To the Tune of Yan Er Mei
(The Eyes' Fascination)
Zhanghua, Taiwan
October 10, 2009

When the terrifying waves
In the Huangpu River
Began to attack the Fishing Boat,
You, Fr. Matthew,
Then a seminarian,
Rose to battle the raging waves.
You were put behind bars
For thirty years;
Your fighting will remained still firm.
Finally,
In going to the United States,
You abounded in joy.

You moved here to Taiwan.
Having studied diligently,
You received the sacred order.
Then you started to write and edit
On the history of the persecuted Church.
You have already published twenty books
To benefit thc people and the country,
To revive the Church
And to glorify Heaven!

265. 訪五嫂家

七絕
台灣宜蘭
羅冬鄉
2009 年 10 月 13 日

雨暴風狂到嫂家，

親人初晤樂無涯。

千言萬語情難盡，

週後西窗剪燭花！

265.   A Visit To The Family Of My Fifth Sister-In-Law

In the Poetic Style of Qijue
In Luodong Township
Yilan, Taiwan
October 13, 2009

In torrential rain and fierce wind,
I come to your home,
Oh, my sister-in-law.
Meeting you, my relatives,
For the first time,
My joy knows no bounds.
A multitude of tender words
Will be unable to express my feelings
In their entirety.
In a week,
I will return
To talk with all of you
So long as to snuff
The candle by the west window
Unceasingly!

266. 拜謁
蔣中正總統慈湖陵寢

臨江仙
台灣桃園
2009 年 10 月 17 日

四合院房陵寢樸，
牆懸遺像靈堂，
雍容靈柩在中央。
哨兵門口駐，
溫厚又端莊。

換哨衛兵交接禮，
整齊俐落堂堂，
圍觀遊客喜洋洋。
待酬興國志，
功績實輝煌！

266.   Paying Homage At The Cihu Mausoleum Of President Jiang Zhongzheng

To the Tune of Lin Jiang Zian
(Immortal by the River)
Taoyuan, Taiwan
October 17, 2009

Being a courtyard house,
The mausoleum is very simple.
In the mourning hall
There are the President's photograph
Hanging on the wall,
And his solemn coffin in the middle.
Stationed at the entrance,
The guards are
Gentle, kind and dignified,

The ceremony of relieving the sentry
Is neat, agile and impressive;
The crowd of
Surrounding and onlooking tourists
Beam with pleasure
In watching the ceremony.
The President's ambitions
Of rejuvenating the nation
Wait to be realized;
His contributions have really been splendid!

267. 遊日月潭

人月圓
台灣南投
2009 年 10 月 19 日

秋高氣爽嬌陽照，
湖泊好風光。
日潭島北，
月潭南面，
同映蟾光。

青山環抱，
翠林圍繞，
碧水泱泱。
乘舟覽勝，
賞心悅目，
謝主君王！

267.   Sightseeing At The Riyuetan (Sun And Moon Lake)

To the Tune of Ren Yue Yuan
(The Family Reunion and the Full Moon)
Nantou, Taiwan
October 19, 2009

On an autumn day,
With gentle sunshine, clear sky and crisp air,
The lake is a beautiful sight.
The Sun Lake to the north of the island
And the Moon Lake to the south,
Both mirror the moonlight.

The lake is surrounded
By green mountains, hills and trees.
It has a vast expanse of blue water.
Touring the scenery in a boat,
I feel flattered in the heart
And pleased in the eye.
I sing my grateful praise
To the Lord, our King!

268. 告別老友
林永明先生

采桑子
台灣中壢市
2009 年 10 月 25 日

加州修院蒙來訪，
念四年前。
豈料今天，
寶島重逢又有緣?!

客居期內承關照，
領路頻繁。
謝惘難言，
但望**天堂**永見歡！

268.   Saying Goodbye
To My Old Friend,
Mr. John-Paul Lin Yongming

To the Tune of Cai Sang Zi
(Picking Mulberries)
Chongli City, Taiwan
October 25, 2009

When you came
To visit our monastery in California,
It was twenty-four years ago.
Today,
How could I expect
That we were once more destined
To meet again in the Precious Island ?!

During my sojourn here,
I have been indebted to you
For your cares,
For your frequently leading my way.
It is hard for me
To express my gratitude to you.
I only wish to see you gladly
In Heaven forever and a day!

269. 拜訪香港苦修會 聖母神樂院

蝶戀花
香港
2009 年 11 月 5 日

海島風光修院享,
鬧市遠離境靜胸開朗。
堂內禱聲霄漢上,
心靈與主相交往。

大陸逃離洵悵惘,
新院建成頌主修身暢。
五十多年光彩放,
凱歌猶待還鄉唱!

269.   Visiting
Our Lady Of Joy Abbey,
A Trappist Monastery
In Hong Kong

To the Tune of Die Lian Hua
(Butterflies Courting Flowers)
Hong Kong
November 5, 2009

Your abbey enjoys the scene of an island.
Far away from busy streets,
It offers a tranquil environment
And may broaden and clear your chest.
Your prayer in the chapel
Ascends to the sky;
Your hearts
Contact with the Lord.

You who had fled from the Mainland
Were truly anxious.
Since having established the new abbey,
You have felt happy
In singing the praises of the Lord
And in cultivating yourselves.
During the last fifty-plus years,
You have given forth your brilliance.
Now,
You may still wait
For singing the triumphant song
Of returning your homeland!

270. 陪伴德肋撒・瑪利亞・莫洛女士領取頒贈給她的新聞特寫《在華與天主同在》的優勝獎

七言詩
聖安德肋大修院
2010 年 6 月 27 日

新聞傑作頌獎宴，
洛市新聞俱樂部，
聖母名城舉辦夜，
數百賓客盛會聚。

百餘佳作蒙青睞，
莫洛特寫亦飲譽；
伴隨登台獎品領，
共同致謝賓與主，

莫文刊於《殘存者》，
客歲三月煙花舞；
《在華與**天主**同在》，
華鐸和已往事敘。

面對**教難**熊熊火，
神聖**信仰**勇衛護；
為**主**恃**主**戰而捷，
終來自由之國度。

戰鬥歷程得追憶，
衛**教**經歷慶刊佈；
喜見引起世回響，
月光照我回院路！

270.   Accompanying Theresa Marie Moreau To Receive First Place Award For Her News Feature, *With God In China*

In the Poetic Style of Qiyan Shi
St. Andrew's Abbey
June 27, 2010

A dinner for handing out awards for excellence
To news masterpieces of the year,
The Los Angeles Press Club
Held at night in the famous city of Our Lady.
Several hundred guests came to the joyous gathering.

More than one hundred fine works
Have won the favor;
The feature by Theresa Marie Moreau has also enjoyed fame.
Having mounted the platform and received the award,
Theresa and I, her companion,
We have shown our gratitude to the guest and host.

Her article was published in *The Remnant*
In March of last year
When the flowers were dancing like smoke.
"*With God In China*"
Narrates the past of our Fr. Eleutherius Winance and me.

Facing the raging fire of the religious persecution,
We bravely defended our sacred Faith.
For the Lord and relying on the Lord,
We combated and scored the victory;
We finally came to this country of freedom!

My fighting course
Was then recalled;
My experiences of defending the Church
Were luckily published.
I am cheerful to see a reverberation in the world.
My way back to the Abbey is bathed in moonlight!

271. 秦麗君小姐
領注蒙市購書

眼兒媚
聖安德肋大修院
2011 年 9 月 5 日

勞工節日棄休閒，
應請慨來援，
領奔蒙市，
購書兩本，
送返平安。

自台遷美多年矣，
工作獨身歡。
虔誠信主，
熱心助眾，
夕照斑斕。

271.   Miss Terry Qin Lijun Leads Me To Monterey Park To Buy Books

To the Tune of Yan Er Mei
(The Eyes' Fascination)
St. Andrew's Abbey
September 5, 2011

At the feast of Labor Day,
You gave up your rest and leisure,
And, at my request,
Came to give me help generously.
You led me to Monterey Park
To buy two books.
You also drove me back safe and sound.

You moved from Taiwan to America
For many years.
You take delight
In working and in living single.
You believe in the Lord devoutly
And help others ardently.
Your face,
Like the setting sun
Glows brightly.

272. 熱烈歡迎
橡樹林小學
本屆五年級畢業生

四言詩
聖安德肋大修院
2011 年 10 月 20 日

良宵盛會，學童歡聚；
載歌載舞，生龍活虎。
賓主問答，井然有序；
交談氣氛，輕鬆和煦。

祝願弟妹，乘勝進取；
升學勤讀，德智培育；
身心鍛鍊，**真善**步武；
善度人生，永見**天父**！

272.   Welcoming Warmly This Year's Graduates, Fifth Graders, From The Oakwood Elementary School

In the Poetic Style of Siyan Shi
St. Andrew's Abbey
October 20, 2011

A happy and pleasant evening,
At a grand party
The pupils come, getting together joyously.
They sing and dance,
Full of vim and vigor,
Like dragons and tigers.
The questions and answers
Between the guests and the hosts
Are carried out orderly;
The atmosphere of conversations
Is light-hearted and genial.

We bid you,
Our young brothers and sisters,
Keepng forging ahead on the crest of a victory;
Going to a higher school,
Sudying diligently,
Cultivating character and intelligence;
Building up the body and the mind,
Pursuing the truth and the goodness;
And ultimately,
Having lived a good life,
Seeng our Heavenly Father forever and ever!

273. 恭賀湯姆和安吉・米勒 榮任終身執事

鵲橋仙
聖安德肋大修院
2011 年 11 月 5 日

多年相識，
熟知往事，
閱讀承蒙拙著。
歷經曲折路人生，
休怨嘆、禧迎兩度！

夕陽臨近，
天成佳偶；
執事還承榮譽。
効勞為**教**為鄰人，
定易進、**天鄉**樂土！

273.   Congratulations To Tom And Angie Miller For The Honor Of Being Ordained To A Permanent Deacon

To the Tune of Que Qiao Xian
(The Magpie Bridge)
St. Andrew's Abbey
November 5, 2011

We have been acquainted with each other
For years.
You knew well my past;
I am appreciative of
Your reading my books.
You have experienced
A tortuous path of life.
You do not complain or sigh for this,
Because you received happiness twice!

While approaching the setting sun,
You have been made perfect matches by Heaven;
You were even just now granted
The honor of a permanent deacon.
When you offer your service
To the Church and to your neighbors,
You will surely and more easily
Enter the Heavenly homeland, the land of happiness!

274. 娟燕遊碧空
—獻給新好友陳燕娟女士—

七言詩
聖安德肋大修院
2011 年 12 月 6 日

十月九日秋光燦，
金風送來好同鄉；
一知愚事見拙著，
動容拍照十二張。

君生湖南剛三歲，
送閩撫養由爹娘；
初中畢業年十四，
負笈河南志氣昂。

讀完軍事醫學院，
服務部隊績效彰；
十一春後上尉銜，
退役前往黃浦江。

274.   A Beautiful Swallow Tours In The Blue Sky
—Dedicated to my new good friend,
Ms. Annie Chen Yanjuan—

In the Poetic Style of Qiyan Shi
St. Andrew's Abbey
December 6, 2011

On October 9,
With a resplendent autumn scene,
The fall wind brought you to me,
As a good countrywoman.
Had you no sooner known my story
And seen my books
Than were visibly moved
And took twelve pictures.

At the age just 3,
After your birth in Hunan,
You were brought to Fujian
To be raised by your parents.
At 14, when you graduated from junior high school,
Carrying your satchel,
You left home for Henan, with high ambition,
To pursue studies.

Having completed your studies
In the military medical academy,
You served in the army
With marked achievements.
Eleven springs later,
As a captain,
Retiring from the active military service,
You went to Huangpu Jiang.

參加「民建」入政協，
從事醫藥展專長。
十一冬後離上海，
越洋來此自由邦。

研製藥品創公司，
偉業加州斯濫觴；
路易志同結連理，
業務重擔齊擔當。

頭四七年如水逝，
後四七年正開航；
認識**真理**信**基督**，
工作生活喜洋洋。

君有美名叫「燕娟」，
君如秀燕碧空翔，
衷心祝願天年滿，
飛越九霄入**天堂**！

You joined in
The China Democratic National Construction Association.
You were also selected as a member to
The Shanghai City Political Consultative Conference.
You showed your special skill
In engaging in the medical work.
You left Shanghai after eleven winters,
And came, across the occean,
Here to the country of freedom.

For researching and producing medicines,
You established a company,
And your great undertaking
Originated thus from here California.
You got married with Mr. Louis Poreider,
A man with the same ideals;
And have taken with him together
On the heavy burden of the company business.

Your first forty-seven years have gone,
Like the flow of water,
And now,
Your next forty-seven years have begun.
If you would like
To know the Truth and believe in Christ,
You may beam with joy in working and in living.

You have a beautiful name, Yanjuan, Beautiful Swallow;
Like a beantiful swallow,
You are flying in the blue sky!
I sincerely wish:
When you reach your alloted span of life,
You will fly beyond the highest heavens
And enter the Paradise!

275. 喜赴
阿曼達・索菲・金小姐
和斯科特・埃撒・
卡爾維特先生的婚禮

人月圓
聖安德肋大修院
2012 年 1 月 28 日

藍天冬日身心暖，
婚典與歡欣。
鐸方主禮，
主前盟誓，
佳偶終身。

伴孃好姊，
椿萱齊悅，
大宴朋親。
夜辭東道，
歸途登上，
餘韻猶存！

275. Joyfully Going To The Wedding Celebration Of Miss Amanda Sophie Kim With Mr. Scott Ethan Calvert

To the Tune of Ren Yue Yuan
(The Family Reunion and the Full Moon)
St. Andrew's Abbey
January 28, 2012

The winter sun in the blue sky
Warms up my body and my nind.
I am joyous to attend the wedding celebration.
Our Fr. Francis Benedict presides over the ceremony;
You, Amanda and Scott,
Swear your oaths to each other
In the presence of the Lord,
And then
You become a happy and lifelong married couple!

O Amanda,
Your good elder sister, Jennifer, is your maid of honor,
And your faher and mother, Paul and Christina,
Are both very glad
And entertain your friends and relatives
Over cocktails and dinner.
Taking leave of the hosts at night,
We, Fr. Francis and I,
Set our feet on the way home
With a remaining aftertaste in our hearts!